W9-AXY-770

see his passion.

sense his presence.

feel his love.

hear his voice.

know the real JESUS.

JESUS BIBLE

Gospel of Mark
SAMPLER

NEW LIVING
TRANSLATION®

TYNDALE HOUSE PUBLISHERS, INC. · WHEATON, ILLINOIS

Visit us at www.newlivingtranslation.com

The Jesus Bible, Gospel of Mark Sampler copyright © 2002 by Tyndale House Publishers, Inc. All rights reserved.

Study notes for *The Jesus Bible* copyright © 2002 by The Livingstone Corporation. All rights reserved.

Devotional material included in this sampler excerpted from the Real Life . . . Real Questions . . . Real Jesus series © 2002 by Standard Publishing, a division of Standex International Corporation, Cincinnati, OH. Devotional samples also include material taken from *The Jesus Bible.*

All Scripture text in this sampler is taken from *Holy Bible,* New Living Translation, copyright © 1996 by Tyndale Charitable Trust. All rights reserved.

The text of the *Holy Bible,* New Living Translation, may be quoted in any form (written, visual, electronic, or audio) up to and inclusive of two hundred and fifty (250) verses without express written permission of the publisher, provided that the verses quoted do not account for more than 20 percent of the work in which they are quoted, and provided that a complete book of the Bible is not quoted.

When the *Holy Bible,* New Living Translation, is quoted, one of the following credit lines must appear on the copyright page or title page of the work:

Scripture quotations marked NLT are taken from the *Holy Bible,* New Living Translation, copyright © 1996. Used by permission of Tyndale House Publishers, Inc., Wheaton, Illinois 60189. All rights reserved.

Scripture quotations are taken from the *Holy Bible,* New Living Translation, copyright © 1996. Used by permission of Tyndale House Publishers, Inc., Wheaton, Illinois 60189. All rights reserved.

Unless otherwise indicated, all Scripture quotations are taken from the *Holy Bible,* New Living Translation, copyright © 1996. Used by permission of Tyndale House Publishers, Inc., Wheaton, Illinois 60189. All rights reserved.

When quotations from the NLT text are used in nonsalable media, such as church bulletins, orders of service, newsletters, transparencies, or similar media, a complete copyright notice is not required, but the initials NLT must appear at the end of each quotation.

Quotations in excess of two hundred and fifty (250) verses or 20 percent of the work, or other permission requests, must be directed to and approved in writing by Tyndale House Publishers, Inc., P.O. Box 80, Wheaton, Illinois 60189.

Publication of any commentary or other Bible reference work produced for commercial sale that uses the New Living Translation requires written permission for use of the NLT text.

New Living Translation and the New Living Translation logo are registered trademarks of Tyndale House Publishers, Inc.

Printed in the United States of America

ISBN 0-8423-7642-9

06   05   04   03   02
7   6   5   4   3   2   1

Each sale of the *Holy Bible,* New Living Translation, benefits Wycliffe Bible Translators, which completed its five hundredth New Testament in 1999 and plans to undertake translation work in every language that needs it by 2025. Tyndale House Publishers and Wycliffe Bible Translators share the vision for an understandable, accurate translation of the Bible for every person.

what's up with the Χ?

For centuries Χ has been a symbol for Christ, the anointed one, the Savior. First-century Christians took the Greek letter Χ (pronounced "ki" or "key"), which is the first letter in the Greek word for Christ (χριστοσ, pronounced "kree-STAS"), and incorporated it into a variety of symbols to represent their faith in Jesus, the one sent from God. The symbol was simple. It pointed to the cross and became a sign identifying believers. The mark and its variations can be found in the ancient Roman catacombs and on early coins, lamps, and pottery.

Today, Χ still stands for Christ. It is the bridge between tradition and a new millennium. As you prepare yourself for the future, you need the right tools to make sense of a world that often appears senseless. You will need answers to the tough questions, such as "Why did God make me the way he did?" and "What is my purpose here on earth?" With so many different voices and opinions from parents, peers, teachers, television, radio, the Internet, and others, you will need a firm foundation on which to make good decisions about *your* life and *your* future.

You will need Jesus—not the watered-down religious pacifist or the timid-looking person in a stained-glass window—but the real Jesus, in all his color, with all his power, showing up in the most unexpected places and taking the most revolutionary actions. *The Jesus Bible* follows Christ from the Old Testament prophecies about him to his life and ministry on earth. It records Jesus' call to radical living, first voiced more than two thousand years ago, that still resounds today. Through *The Jesus Bible*, you will encounter the real Jesus for real life with real answers for life's tough problems.

Χ One symbol. One man. One God. One Truth. One hope. He's all you'll ever need.

the unXpected Gift

Whether they are stuffed in a huge box with a big red bow, wrapped in shiny paper in a tiny package, or delivered by mail in an envelope, gifts are wonderful to receive. Whatever the occasion, we enthusiastically tear through the wrappings to find out what's inside. We expect to receive gifts on birthdays, at Christmas, and on special occasions like graduations and anniversaries. But receiving a totally unexpected gift—that's a real bonus.

Here's great news: You are eligible to receive the greatest, most unexpected gift ever.

what is the gift?

"For God so loved the world that he gave his only Son, so that everyone who believes in him will not perish but have eternal life" (John 3:16). Did you catch that? God loves *you* so much that he sent his son, Jesus, to the earth to save you. Through Jesus, you can receive eternal life and have a relationship with the Creator of the universe (John 17:3). That's the greatest gift ever given to anyone in all history.

why do we need it?

So what's the big deal about this gift? Good question. In a word, the answer is sin. According to the Bible, everyone who is breathing sins (Romans 3:23). What is sin? Basically, it's doing what is wrong (1 John 3:4) and not doing what is right (James 4:17). Sin includes lying, stealing, and murdering, but it also includes what we say, think, or do that goes against what God commands. So everyone sins every day.

The big problem with sin is that it separates us from God. Because God is perfect, he can't allow sin in his presence. So unless something happens to change our situation, we're lost, cut off, doomed. "But there is a problem—your sins have cut you off from God. Because of your sin, he has turned away and will not listen anymore" (Isaiah 59:2).

Only through Jesus, God's unexpected and perfect gift, can we have a relationship with the holy God (See John 14:6). By offering himself as the perfect sacrifice, Jesus paid the penalty for our sin on the cross. "Christ also suffered when he died for our sins once for all time. He never sinned, but he died for sinners that he might bring us safely home to God" (1 Peter 3:18).

so how do we get this gift?

To receive this gift, you just need to accept it. You do that by taking these three important steps:

1) Turn from your sin. "Now turn from your sins and turn to God, so you can be cleansed of your sins" (Acts 3:19). This means telling God you are sorry for doing, saying, or thinking whatever is not pleasing to him.

2) Trust in Jesus. "*We are made right in God's sight when we trust in Jesus Christ to take away our sins. And we all can be saved in this same way, no matter who we are or what we have done*" (Romans 3:22). *In this step, thank God for sending his Son to die on the cross in your place, taking the penalty for your sins.*

3) Receive Christ as your Savior. "*But to all who believed him and accepted him, he gave the right to become children of God*" (John 1:12). *This means asking God to come into your life and take control and committing yourself to God.*

what's next?

By accepting this gift, you become God's very own child (1 John 3:1). So here's what to do next. These steps will help your relationship with God grow deeper.

1) Tell someone! Tell a parent, a youth pastor, or a friend about your gift and how you received it. This person should be someone who can help you along this exciting new faith journey.

2) Begin reading God's Word (the Bible). This will help you learn more about God and his plan for you. Several reading plans are included in the back of this Bible to help you get started.

3) Talk daily to God through prayer. There is no issue too big or too small for God to handle. Bring all your concerns to him in prayer, and he will listen. "*Don't worry about anything; instead, pray about everything. Tell God what you need, and thank him for all he has done*" (Philippians 4:6).

4) Finally, celebrate! You have just received a gift that will never fade, break down, or wear out; it's a gift that will last forever. "*So now we can rejoice in our wonderful new relationship with God—all because of what our Lord Jesus Christ has done for us in making us friends of God*" (Romans 5:11).

HOW TO USE THE JESUS BIBLE

Welcome to *The Jesus Bible!* If you wonder who Jesus really is, we hope that through this Bible you will discover his true identity, why he came, and what he did for you. If you already have a relationship with Christ, we hope that you will discover in new, fresh, and unexpected ways what an incredible Master, Teacher, Savior, and Friend you have in him. Whatever your situation, we hope that the notes and features in this Bible will point you to the Way, the Truth, and the Life.

The following is a quick look at the features and notes you will find in *The Jesus Bible*.

XFOCUS
Let these short statements or questions bring you face-to-face with God's truth and what it means for you today.

unXpected
Meet the *real* Jesus through these notes highlighting the unexpected situations, relationships, and conversations that feature Christ. Jesus will surprise you with where he appears, what he does, and who he chooses as friends.

ReaL Xpressions
See yourself in these stories based on real-life experiences from stealing to parents divorcing to dealing with a best friend who just announced he's gay. Discover that Jesus has something relevant, hopeful, and wise to say about the struggles you face.

XpLicit Answers
Find the Bible's answers to tough questions, such as: "How do you answer a friend who believes that any god will do?" or "Who wants to know if God is so good, why does he allow evil in the world?" These full-page articles provide real answers to issues dealing with Jesus, the Christian faith, the Bible, and lifestyles.

Jesus XcLaims
Learn what Jesus has to say about money, divorce, life after death, and other topics. Jesus' quotes are tied to Scripture throughout the Bible.

Xtraordinary
Gain a new perspective on God's Word through these notes that highlight intriguing stories, customs, and events throughout the Bible. Through these extraordinary accounts, you'll discover just how far God will go to pursue individuals, to interact in this world, and to show mercy and love to his people.

XpLore
Check out the book introductions to get an overview of each book, to see how Jesus is featured in the book, and to understand how each book is part of one story—God's plan of salvation through his Son.

Xalt Him

Explore the person of Jesus Christ—his humanity, his deity, his purpose, and his character—through the variety of names, titles, and descriptions used to identify him in the Bible. Find out how each name highlights an unique aspect of Jesus' mission and personality and what that means for you.

mark

Our culture is set to hyperspeed. We want our food fast, our movies action-packed, and our ability to communicate at the click of a computer mouse. The Gospel writer, Mark, would have felt at home in our world.

Mark's Gospel, the shortest and simplest of the four, follows Jesus' ministry through one action-packed event after another. Mark took some, not all, of the significant events surrounding the person and work of Jesus and built his Gospel around them.

Like the other Gospel writers, Mark wrote with a certain emphasis and for a specific audience. Writing to Roman believers, Mark highlighted Jesus as a servant-leader. His readers were likely very practical, and they wanted to know why Jesus came and why he had to die. Mark's Gospel demonstrates that Jesus is the ultimate servant, whose greatest act of service was to give his life so that his people could be forgiven.

WHO WROTE MARK?
Although the author of this Gospel is never explicitly stated, the early church leaders unanimously attributed this book to Mark, also known as John Mark. Mark was not a disciple, but he accompanied Paul on his first missionary journey along with his cousin Barnabas. Later, Mark most likely served as interpreter for Peter and recorded various things that Peter remembered about Jesus' life, ministry, and teachings. Mark wrote this fast-paced account of Jesus' life to a Roman audience. Mark was intent on demonstrating to a culture that worshiped many gods that Jesus was, and is, the true Son of God.

SPOTLIGHT ON JESUS
Mark's audience, the Romans, saw Jesus primarily as a problem for the Jewish leaders, and later, as a crucified criminal. They weren't as concerned with Jesus' Jewish heritage or the Old Testament prophecies surrounding him. So Mark emphasized that Jesus came to actively serve people by meeting all their needs.

That's why much of this Gospel concentrates on Jesus' miracles. Mark was more concerned about showing what Jesus did than what Jesus said. Mark also battled the perception that Jesus had been a criminal. After all, a Roman governor had sentenced Jesus to death. Mark showed this was the ultimate act of servanthood—obediently, willingly, and compassionately giving his life for others.

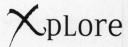
XpLore

1
John the Baptist Prepares the Way
Here begins the Good News about Jesus the Messiah, the Son of God.* [2]In the book of the prophet Isaiah, God said,

"Look, I am sending my messenger before you,
and he will prepare your way.*
[3]He is a voice shouting in the wilderness:
'Prepare a pathway for the Lord's coming!
Make a straight road for him!'*"

[4]This messenger was John the Baptist. He lived in the wilderness and was preaching that people should be baptized to show that they had turned from their sins and turned to God to be forgiven.* [5]People from Jerusalem and from all over Judea traveled out into the wilderness to see and hear John. And when they confessed their sins, he baptized them in the Jordan River. [6]His clothes were woven from camel hair, and he wore a leather belt; his food was locusts and wild honey. [7]He announced: "Someone is coming soon who is far greater than I am—so much greater that I am not even worthy to be his slave.* [8]I baptize you with* water, but he will baptize you with the Holy Spirit!"

what John started, Jesus finished. what John prepared, Jesus completed. (1:7-8)

The Baptism of Jesus
[9]One day Jesus came from Nazareth in Galilee, and he was baptized by John in the Jordan River. [10]And when Jesus came up out of the water, he saw the heavens split open and the Holy Spirit descending like a dove on him. [11]And a voice came from heaven saying, "You are my beloved Son, and I am fully pleased with you."

The Temptation of Jesus
[12]Immediately the Holy Spirit compelled Jesus to go into the wilderness. [13]He was there for forty days, being tempted by Satan. He was out among the wild animals, and angels took care of him.

The First Disciples
[14]Later on, after John was arrested by Herod Antipas, Jesus went to Galilee to preach God's Good News. [15]"At last the time has come!" he announced. "The Kingdom of God is near! Turn from your sins and believe this Good News!"

[16]One day as Jesus was walking along the shores of the Sea of Galilee, he saw Simon* and his brother, Andrew, fishing with a net, for they were commercial fishermen. [17]Jesus called out to them, "Come, be my disciples, and I will show you how to fish for people!" [18]And they left their nets at once and went with him.

[19]A little farther up the shore Jesus saw Zebedee's sons, James and John, in a boat mending their nets. [20]He called them, too, and immediately they left their father, Zebedee, in the boat with the hired men and went with him.

Jesus Casts Out an Evil Spirit
[21]Jesus and his companions went to the town of Capernaum, and every Sabbath day he went into the synagogue and taught the people. [22]They were amazed at his teaching, for he taught as one who had real authority—quite unlike the teachers of religious law.

[23]A man possessed by an evil spirit was in the synagogue, [24]and he began shouting, "Why are you bothering us, Jesus of Nazareth? Have you come to destroy us? I know who you are—the Holy One sent from God!"

[25]Jesus cut him short. "Be silent! Come out of the man." [26]At that, the evil spirit screamed and threw the man into a convulsion, but then he left him.

[27]Amazement gripped the audience, and they began to discuss what had happened. "What sort of new teaching is this?" they asked excitedly. "It has such authority! Even evil spirits obey his orders!" [28]The news of what he had done spread quickly through that entire area of Galilee.

Jesus Heals Many People
[29]After Jesus and his disciples left the synagogue, they went over to Simon and Andrew's home, and James and John were with them.

1:1 Some manuscripts do not include *the Son of God.* 1:2 Mal 3:1. 1:3 Isa 40:3. 1:4 Greek *preaching a baptism of repentance for the forgiveness of sins.* 1:7 Greek *to stoop down and untie his sandals.* 1:8 Or *in;* also in 1:8b. 1:16 *Simon* is called *Peter* in 3:16 and thereafter.

³⁰Simon's mother-in-law was sick in bed with a high fever. They told Jesus about her right away. ³¹He went to her bedside, and as he took her by the hand and helped her to sit up, the fever suddenly left, and she got up and prepared a meal for them.

³²That evening at sunset, many sick and demon-possessed people were brought to Jesus. ³³And a huge crowd of people from all over Capernaum gathered outside the door to watch. ³⁴So Jesus healed great numbers of sick people who had many different kinds of diseases, and he ordered many demons to come out of their victims. But because they knew who he was, he refused to allow the demons to speak.

Jesus Preaches in Galilee

³⁵The next morning Jesus awoke long before daybreak and went out alone into the wilderness to pray. ³⁶Later Simon and the others went out to find him. ³⁷They said, "Everyone is asking for you."

³⁸But he replied, "We must go on to other towns as well, and I will preach to them, too, because that is why I came." ³⁹So he traveled throughout the region of Galilee, preaching in the synagogues and expelling demons from many people.

1:41 Some manuscripts read *Moved with anger.*

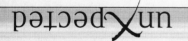

Jesus tells his followers to go fish for others. The hook? Faith in a Living God. (1:17)

Jesus Heals a Man with Leprosy

⁴⁰A man with leprosy came and knelt in front of Jesus, begging to be healed. "If you want to, you can make me well again," he said.

⁴¹Moved with pity,* Jesus touched him. "I want to," he said. "Be healed!" ⁴²Instantly the leprosy disappeared—the man was healed. ⁴³Then Jesus sent him on his way and told him sternly, ⁴⁴"Go right over to the priest and let him examine you. Don't talk to anyone along the way. Take along the offering required in the law of Moses for those who have been healed of leprosy, so everyone will have proof of your healing."

⁴⁵But as the man went on his way, he spread the news, telling everyone what had happened to him. As a result, such crowds soon surrounded Jesus that he couldn't enter a town anywhere publicly. He had to stay out in the secluded places, and people from everywhere came to him there.

unexpected

AT THE BEACH

We don't typically think of beaches as being sites of profound spirituality. People party at the beach. They drink, wear skimpy bathing suits, read trashy novels, and engage in other types of mindless, often immoral behavior.

Yet it was on a beach that Jesus encountered his first disciples. They were fishing, and so was Jesus—for followers. Little did Peter and Andrew know that when they walked away from their boats and nets, they were embarking on the wildest adventure of their lives.

In seeking us, Jesus comes to where we are. If that happens to be a beach, then a beach—or wherever he finds us—is where we can meet Jesus and be forever changed.

MARK 1:16-18

Jesus knew talk is cheap. He backed up his heavenly claims with earthly miracles. (2:10-12)

2 Jesus Heals a Paralyzed Man

Several days later Jesus returned to Capernaum, and the news of his arrival spread quickly through the town. ²Soon the house where he was staying was so packed with visitors that there wasn't room for one more person, not even outside the door. And he preached the word to them. ³Four men arrived carrying a paralyzed man on a mat. ⁴They couldn't get to Jesus through the crowd, so they dug through the clay roof above his head. Then they lowered the sick man on his mat, right down in front of Jesus. ⁵Seeing their faith, Jesus said to the paralyzed man, "My son, your sins are forgiven."

⁶But some of the teachers of religious law who were sitting there said to themselves, ⁷"What? This is blasphemy! Who but God can forgive sins!"

⁸Jesus knew what they were discussing among themselves, so he said to them, "Why do you think this is blasphemy? ⁹Is it easier to say to the paralyzed man, 'Your sins are forgiven' or 'Get up, pick up your mat, and walk'? ¹⁰I will prove that I, the Son of Man, have the authority on earth to forgive sins." Then Jesus turned to the paralyzed man and said, ¹¹"Stand up, take your mat, and go on home, because you are healed!"

¹²The man jumped up, took the mat, and pushed his way through the stunned onlookers. Then they all praised God. "We've never seen anything like this before!" they exclaimed.

Jesus Calls Levi (Matthew)

¹³Then Jesus went out to the lakeshore again and taught the crowds that gathered around him. ¹⁴As he walked along, he saw Levi son of Alphaeus sitting at his tax-collection booth. "Come, be my disciple," Jesus said to him. So Levi got up and followed him.

¹⁵That night Levi invited Jesus and his disciples to be his dinner guests, along with his fellow tax collectors and many other notorious sinners. (There were many people of this kind among the crowds that followed Jesus.) ¹⁶But when some of the teachers of religious law who were Pharisees* saw him eating with people like that, they said to his disciples, "Why does he eat with such scum*?"

¹⁷When Jesus heard this, he told them, "Healthy people don't need a doctor—sick people do. I have come to call sinners, not those who think they are already good enough."

A Discussion about Fasting

¹⁸John's disciples and the Pharisees sometimes fasted. One day some people came to Jesus and asked, "Why do John's disciples and the Pharisees fast, but your disciples don't fast?"

¹⁹Jesus replied, "Do wedding guests fast while celebrating with the groom? Of course not. They can't fast while they are with the groom. ²⁰But someday he will be taken away from them, and then they will fast. ²¹And who would patch an old garment with unshrunk cloth? For the new patch shrinks and pulls away from the old cloth, leaving an even bigger hole than before. ²²And no one puts new wine into old wineskins. The wine would burst the wineskins, spilling the wine and ruining the skins. New wine needs new wineskins."

A Discussion about the Sabbath

²³One Sabbath day as Jesus was walking through some grainfields, his disciples began breaking off heads of wheat. ²⁴But the Pharisees said to Jesus, "They shouldn't be doing that! It's against the law to work by harvesting grain on the Sabbath."

²⁵But Jesus replied, "Haven't you ever read in the Scriptures what King David did when he and his companions were hungry? ²⁶He went into the house of God (during the days when Abiathar was high priest), ate the special bread

Don't let old ideas and prejudices keep you from new life in Jesus. (2:19-22)

2:16a Greek *the scribes of the Pharisees.* 2:16b Greek *with tax collectors and sinners.*

reserved for the priests alone, and then gave some to his companions. That was breaking the law, too." ²⁷Then he said to them, "The Sabbath was made to benefit people, and not people to benefit the Sabbath. ²⁸And I, the Son of Man, am master even of the Sabbath!"

3

Jesus Heals on the Sabbath

Jesus went into the synagogue again and noticed a man with a deformed hand. ²Since it was the Sabbath, Jesus' enemies watched him closely. Would he heal the man's hand on the Sabbath? If he did, they planned to condemn him. ³Jesus said to the man, "Come and stand in front of everyone." ⁴Then he turned to his critics and asked, "Is it legal to do good deeds on the Sabbath, or is it a day for doing harm? Is this a day to save life or to destroy it?" But they wouldn't answer him. ⁵He looked around at them angrily, because he was deeply disturbed by their hard hearts. Then he said to the man, "Reach out your hand." The man reached out his hand, and it became normal again! ⁶At once the Pharisees went away and met with the supporters of Herod to discuss plans for killing Jesus.

Crowds Follow Jesus

⁷Jesus and his disciples went out to the lake, followed by a huge crowd from all over Gali- lee, Judea, ⁸Jerusalem, Idumea, from east of the Jordan River, and even from as far away as Tyre and Sidon. The news about his miracles had spread far and wide, and vast numbers of people came to see him for themselves.

⁹Jesus instructed his disciples to bring around a boat and to have it ready in case he was crowded off the beach. ¹⁰There had been many healings that day. As a result, many sick people were crowding around him, trying to touch him. ¹¹And whenever those possessed by evil spirits caught sight of him, they would fall down in front of him shrieking, "You are the Son of God!" ¹²But Jesus strictly warned them not to say who he was.

Jesus Chooses the Twelve Apostles

¹³Afterward Jesus went up on a mountain and called the ones he wanted to go with him. And they came to him. ¹⁴Then he selected twelve of them to be his regular companions, calling them apostles.* He sent them out to preach, ¹⁵and he gave them authority to cast out demons. ¹⁶These are the names of the twelve he chose:

Simon (he renamed him Peter),
¹⁷ James and John (the sons of Zebedee,
but Jesus nicknamed them "Sons
of Thunder"*),
¹⁸ Andrew,

3:14 Some manuscripts do not include *calling them apostles.* **3:17** Greek *whom he named Boanerges, which means Sons of Thunder.*

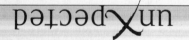

THE GREAT FORGIVER

Imagine walking around your town telling people "Your sins are forgiven!" The response would be one of outrage: "Who do you think you are—God? Only *he* can make such a statement!" Folks would regard you as either supremely arrogant or utterly crazy—and they would be right!

But this is precisely what Jesus went around doing. And in the face of angry opposition, Jesus demonstrated his authority to cancel out sin by doing *bona fide* miracles.

So the big question is: Have you ever let Jesus forgive *your* sins? He came to seek and save those whose souls are sick with sin (Luke 19:10).

MARK 2:5

Philip,
Bartholomew,
Matthew,
Thomas,
James (son of Alphaeus),
Thaddaeus,
Simon (the Zealot*),
¹⁹ Judas Iscariot (who later betrayed him).

Jesus and the Prince of Demons

²⁰When Jesus returned to the house where he was staying, the crowds began to gather again, and soon he and his disciples couldn't even find time to eat. ²¹When his family heard what was happening, they tried to take him home with them. "He's out of his mind," they said.

²²But the teachers of religious law who had arrived from Jerusalem said, "He's possessed by Satan,* the prince of demons. That's where he gets the power to cast out demons."

²³Jesus called them over and said to them by way of illustration, "How can Satan cast out Satan? ²⁴A kingdom at war with itself will collapse. ²⁵A home divided against itself is doomed. ²⁶And if Satan is fighting against himself, how can he stand? He would never survive. ²⁷Let me illustrate this. You can't enter a strong man's house and rob him without first tying him up. Only then can his house be robbed!*

²⁸"I assure you that any sin can be forgiven, including blasphemy; ²⁹but anyone who blasphemes against the Holy Spirit will never be forgiven. It is an eternal sin." ³⁰He told them this because they were saying he had an evil spirit.

The True Family of Jesus

³¹Jesus' mother and brothers arrived at the house where he was teaching. They stood outside and sent word for him to come out and talk with them. ³²There was a crowd around Jesus, and someone said, "Your mother and your brothers and sisters* are outside, asking for you."

³³Jesus replied, "Who is my mother? Who are my brothers?" ³⁴Then he looked at those around him and said, "These are my mother and brothers. ³⁵Anyone who does God's will is my brother and sister and mother."

> It doesn't matter whether you're a master Bible scholar or just a beginner. God expects you to use what you do know. (4:25)

4

Story of the Farmer Scattering Seed

Once again Jesus began teaching by the lakeshore. There was such a large crowd along the shore that he got into a boat and sat down and spoke from there. ²He began to teach the people by telling many stories such as this one:

³"Listen! A farmer went out to plant some seed. ⁴As he scattered it across his field, some seed fell on a footpath, and the birds came and ate it. ⁵Other seed fell on shallow soil with underlying rock. The plant sprang up quickly, ⁶but it soon wilted beneath the hot sun and died because the roots had no nourishment in the shallow soil. ⁷Other seed fell among thorns that shot up and choked out the tender blades so that it produced no grain. ⁸Still other seed fell on fertile soil and produced a crop that was thirty, sixty, and even a hundred times as much as had been planted." Then he said, ⁹"Anyone who is willing to hear should listen and understand!"

¹⁰Later, when Jesus was alone with the twelve disciples and with the others who were gathered around, they asked him, "What do your stories mean?"

¹¹He replied, "You are permitted to understand the secret about the Kingdom of God. But I am using these stories to conceal everything about it from outsiders, ¹²so that the Scriptures might be fulfilled:

'They see what I do,
  but they don't perceive its meaning.
They hear my words,
  but they don't understand.
So they will not turn from their sins
  and be forgiven.'*

¹³"But if you can't understand this story,

3:18 Greek *the Cananean.* **3:22** Greek *Beelzeboul.* **3:27** Or *One cannot rob Satan's kingdom without first tying him up. Only then can his demons be cast out.* **3:32** Some manuscripts do not include *and sisters.* **4:12** Isa 6:9-10.

how will you understand all the others I am going to tell? ¹⁴The farmer I talked about is the one who brings God's message to others. ¹⁵The seed that fell on the hard path represents those who hear the message, but then Satan comes at once and takes it away from them. ¹⁶The rocky soil represents those who hear the message and receive it with joy. ¹⁷But like young plants in such soil, their roots don't go very deep. At first they get along fine, but they wilt as soon as they have problems or are persecuted because they believe the word. ¹⁸The thorny ground represents those who hear and accept the Good News, ¹⁹but all too quickly the message is crowded out by the cares of this life, the lure of wealth, and the desire for nice things, so no crop is produced. ²⁰But the good soil represents those who hear and accept God's message and produce a huge harvest—thirty, sixty, or even a hundred times as much as had been planted."

Illustration of the Lamp

²¹Then Jesus asked them, "Would anyone light a lamp and then put it under a basket or under a bed to shut out the light? Of course not! A lamp is placed on a stand, where its light will shine.

²²"Everything that is now hidden or secret will eventually be brought to light. ²³Anyone who is willing to hear should listen and understand! ²⁴And be sure to pay attention to what you hear. The more you do this, the more you will understand—and even more, besides. ²⁵To those who are open to my teaching, more understanding will be given. But to those who are not listening, even what they have will be taken away from them."

Illustration of the Growing Seed

²⁶Jesus also said, "Here is another illustration of what the Kingdom of God is like: A farmer planted seeds in a field, ²⁷and then he went on with his other activities. As the days went by, the seeds sprouted and grew without the farmer's help, ²⁸because the earth produces crops on its own. First a leaf blade pushes through, then the heads of wheat are formed, and finally the grain ripens. ²⁹And as soon as the grain is ready, the farmer comes and harvests it with a sickle."

Illustration of the Mustard Seed

³⁰Jesus asked, "How can I describe the Kingdom of God? What story should I use to illustrate it? ³¹It is like a tiny mustard seed. Though this is one of the smallest of seeds, ³²it grows to become one of the largest of plants, with long branches where birds can come and find shelter."

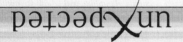

RIGHTEOUS ANGER

"Gentle Jesus, meek and mild" goes the old hymn, adding to our image of Christ as a kind of mamby-pamby Messiah, walking around patting people on the hand and saying, "There, there."

Then suddenly, unexpectedly, we come to the shocking scene of Jesus staring angrily at the Pharisees. He's in a synagogue of all places, on the Sabbath. Yet he's practically smoldering. What gives?

Jesus was angry about the Pharisees' lack of compassion and obsession with man-made rules. It's not a sin to feel angry (Ephesians 4:26). Anger becomes wrong when we're angry about the wrong things or when we act on our anger in harmful ways. Jesus channeled his anger here toward something positive—restoring a sick man to health.

MARK 3:5

when Life's storms hit, remember that Jesus can quiet the wind and calm the seas. (4:39)

[33]He used many such stories and illustrations to teach the people as much as they were able to understand. [34]In fact, in his public teaching he taught only with parables, but afterward when he was alone with his disciples, he explained the meaning to them.

Jesus Calms the Storm

[35]As evening came, Jesus said to his disciples, "Let's cross to the other side of the lake." [36]He was already in the boat, so they started out, leaving the crowds behind (although other boats followed). [37]But soon a fierce storm arose. High waves began to break into the boat until it was nearly full of water.

[38]Jesus was sleeping at the back of the boat with his head on a cushion. Frantically they woke him up, shouting, "Teacher, don't you even care that we are going to drown?"

[39]When he woke up, he rebuked the wind and said to the water, "Quiet down!" Suddenly the wind stopped, and there was a great calm. [40]And he asked them, "Why are you so afraid? Do you still not have faith in me?"

[41]And they were filled with awe and said among themselves, "Who is this man, that even the wind and waves obey him?"

5

Jesus Heals a Demon-Possessed Man

So they arrived at the other side of the lake, in the land of the Gerasenes.* [2]Just as Jesus was climbing from the boat, a man possessed by an evil spirit ran out from a cemetery to meet him. [3]This man lived among the tombs and could not be restrained, even with a chain. [4]Whenever he was put into chains and shackles—as he often was—he snapped the chains from his wrists and smashed the shackles. No one was strong enough to control him. [5]All day long and throughout the night, he would wander among the tombs and in the hills, screaming and hitting himself with stones.

[6]When Jesus was still some distance away, the man saw him. He ran to meet Jesus and fell down before him. [7]He gave a terrible scream, shrieking, "Why are you bothering me, Jesus, Son of the Most High God? For God's sake, don't torture me!" [8]For Jesus had already said to the spirit, "Come out of the man, you evil spirit."

[9]Then Jesus asked, "What is your name?"

And the spirit replied, "Legion, because there are many of us here inside this man." [10]Then the spirits begged him again and again not to send them to some distant place. [11]There happened to be a large herd of pigs feeding on the hillside nearby. [12]"Send us into those pigs," the evil spirits begged. [13]Jesus gave them permission. So the evil spirits came out of the man and entered the pigs, and the entire herd of two thousand pigs plunged down the steep hillside into the lake, where they drowned.

[14]The herdsmen fled to the nearby city and the surrounding countryside, spreading the news as they ran. Everyone rushed out to see for themselves. [15]A crowd soon gathered around Jesus, but they were frightened when they saw the man who had been demon possessed, for he was sitting there fully clothed and perfectly sane. [16]Those who had seen what happened to the man and to the pigs told everyone about it, [17]and the crowd began pleading with Jesus to go away and leave them alone.

[18]When Jesus got back into the boat, the man who had been demon possessed begged to go, too. [19]But Jesus said, "No, go home to your friends, and tell them what wonderful things the Lord has done for you and how merciful he has been." [20]So the man started off to visit the Ten Towns* of that region and began to tell everyone about the great things Jesus had done for him; and everyone was amazed at what he told them.

Jesus Heals in Response to Faith

[21]When Jesus went back across to the other side of the lake, a large crowd gathered around him on the shore. [22]A leader of the local synagogue, whose name was Jairus, came and fell down before him, [23]pleading with him to heal his little daughter. "She is about

5:1 Some manuscripts read *Gadarenes*; others read *Gergesenes*. See Matt 8:28; Luke 8:26. 5:20 Greek *Decapolis*.

to die," he said in desperation. "Please come and place your hands on her; heal her so she can live."

²⁴Jesus went with him, and the crowd thronged behind. ²⁵And there was a woman in the crowd who had had a hemorrhage for twelve years. ²⁶She had suffered a great deal from many doctors through the years and had spent everything she had to pay them, but she had gotten no better. In fact, she was worse. ²⁷She had heard about Jesus, so she came up behind him through the crowd and touched the fringe of his robe. ²⁸For she thought to herself, "If I can just touch his clothing, I will be healed." ²⁹Immediately the bleeding stopped, and she could feel that she had been healed!

³⁰Jesus realized at once that healing power had gone out from him, so he turned around in the crowd and asked, "Who touched my clothes?"

³¹His disciples said to him, "All this crowd is pressing around you. How can you ask, 'Who touched me?'"

³²But he kept on looking around to see who had done it. ³³Then the frightened woman, trembling at the realization of what had happened to her, came and fell at his feet and told him what she had done. ³⁴And he said to her, "Daughter, your faith has made you well. Go in peace. You have been healed."

³⁵While he was still speaking to her, messengers arrived from Jairus's home with the message, "Your daughter is dead. There's no use troubling the Teacher now."

³⁶But Jesus ignored their comments and said to Jairus, "Don't be afraid. Just trust me." ³⁷Then Jesus stopped the crowd and wouldn't let anyone go with him except Peter and James and John. ³⁸When they came to the home of the synagogue leader, Jesus saw the commotion and the weeping and wailing. ³⁹He went inside and spoke to the people. "Why all this weeping and commotion?" he asked. "The child isn't dead; she is only asleep."

⁴⁰The crowd laughed at him, but he told them all to go outside. Then he took the girl's father and mother and his three disciples into the room where the girl was lying. ⁴¹Holding her hand, he said to her, "Get up, little girl!"* ⁴²And the girl, who was twelve years old, immediately stood up and walked around! Her parents were absolutely overwhelmed. ⁴³Jesus commanded them not to tell anyone what had happened, and he told them to give her something to eat.

5:41 Greek text uses Aramaic *"Talitha cumi"* and then translates it as "Get up, little girl."

unexpected

SLOW GOING

In a day of special effects, instant *everything*, and giant extravaganzas, most people seem to prefer a faith that promises spectacular experiences. *Immediate* life change, *radical* healings, *stunning* miracles—we want to hear about these things.

And God does still choose to do such wonders sometimes.

But look again at the parable of Jesus—the one about the growing seed. There he describes a slow, unspectacular, often hard process. The lesson: Don't be disappointed if you see only gradual growth in your life. Whether such change and fruitfulness takes place in a moment or over a long time, it's still a miracle!

MARK 4:26-29

6

Jesus Rejected at Nazareth

Jesus left that part of the country and returned with his disciples to Nazareth, his hometown. [2]The next Sabbath he began teaching in the synagogue, and many who heard him were astonished. They asked, "Where did he get all his wisdom and the power to perform such miracles? [3]He's just the carpenter, the son of Mary and brother of James, Joseph,* Judas, and Simon. And his sisters live right here among us." They were deeply offended and refused to believe in him.

[4]Then Jesus told them, "A prophet is honored everywhere except in his own hometown and among his relatives and his own family." [5]And because of their unbelief, he couldn't do any mighty miracles among them except to place his hands on a few sick people and heal them. [6]And he was amazed at their unbelief.

Jesus Sends Out the Twelve Apostles

Then Jesus went out from village to village, teaching. [7]And he called his twelve disciples together and sent them out two by two, with authority to cast out evil spirits. [8]He told them to take nothing with them except a walking stick—no food, no traveler's bag, no money. [9]He told them to wear sandals but not to take even an extra coat. [10]"When you enter each village, be a guest in only one home," he said. [11]"And if a village won't welcome you or listen to you, shake off its dust from your feet as you leave. It is a sign that you have abandoned that village to its fate."

[12]So the disciples went out, telling all they met to turn from their sins. [13]And they cast out many demons and healed many sick people, anointing them with olive oil.

The Death of John the Baptist

[14]Herod Antipas, the king, soon heard about Jesus, because people everywhere were talking about him. Some were saying,* "This must be John the Baptist come back to life again. That is why he can do such miracles." [15]Others thought Jesus was the ancient prophet Elijah. Still others thought he was a prophet like the other great prophets of the past. [16]When Herod heard about Jesus, he said, "John, the man I beheaded, has come back from the dead." [17]For Herod had sent soldiers to arrest and imprison John as a favor to Herodias. She had been his brother Philip's wife, but Herod had married her. [18]John kept telling Herod, "It is illegal for you to marry your brother's wife." [19]Herodias was enraged and wanted John killed in revenge, but without Herod's approval she was powerless. [20]And Herod respected John, knowing that he was a good and holy man, so he kept him under his protection. Herod was disturbed whenever he talked with John, but even so, he liked to listen to him.

[21]Herodias's chance finally came. It was Herod's birthday, and he gave a party for his palace aides, army officers, and the leading citizens of Galilee. [22]Then his daughter, also named Herodias,* came in and performed a dance that greatly pleased them all. "Ask me for anything you like," the king said to the girl, "and I will give it to you." [23]Then he promised, "I will give you whatever you ask, up to half of my kingdom!"

[24]She went out and asked her mother, "What should I ask for?"

Her mother told her, "Ask for John the Baptist's head!"

[25]So the girl hurried back to the king and told him, "I want the head of John the Baptist, right now, on a tray!"

[26]Then the king was very sorry, but he was embarrassed to break his oath in front of his guests. [27]So he sent an executioner to the prison to cut off John's head and bring it to him. The soldier beheaded John in the prison, [28]brought his head on a tray, and gave it to the girl, who took it to her mother. [29]When John's disciples heard what had happened, they came for his body and buried it in a tomb.

Get over it! when others reject you because of Jesus, it's their problem, not yours. (6:11)

6:3 Greek Joses; see Matt 13:55. 6:14 Some manuscripts read He was saying. 6:22 Some manuscripts read the daughter of Herodias herself.

Jesus Feeds Five Thousand

[30]The apostles returned to Jesus from their ministry tour and told him all they had done and what they had taught. [31]Then Jesus said, "Let's get away from the crowds for a while and rest." There were so many people coming and going that Jesus and his apostles didn't even have time to eat. [32]They left by boat for a quieter spot. [33]But many people saw them leaving, and people from many towns ran ahead along the shore and met them as they landed. [34]A vast crowd was there as he stepped from the boat, and he had compassion on them because they were like sheep without a shepherd. So he taught them many things.

[35]Late in the afternoon his disciples came to him and said, "This is a desolate place, and it is getting late. [36]Send the crowds away so they can go to the nearby farms and villages and buy themselves some food."

[37]But Jesus said, "You feed them."

"With what?" they asked. "It would take a small fortune* to buy food for all this crowd!"

[38]"How much food do you have?" he asked. "Go and find out."

They came back and reported, "We have five loaves of bread and two fish." [39]Then Jesus told the crowd to sit down in groups on

Look past the impossible to God. With him, all things are possible. (6:41-44)

the green grass. [40]So they sat in groups of fifty or a hundred.

[41]Jesus took the five loaves and two fish, looked up toward heaven, and asked God's blessing on the food. Breaking the loaves into pieces, he kept giving the bread and fish to the disciples to give to the people. [42]They all ate as much as they wanted, [43]and they picked up twelve baskets of leftover bread and fish. [44]Five thousand men had eaten from those five loaves!

Jesus Walks on Water

[45]Immediately after this, Jesus made his disciples get back into the boat and head out across the lake to Bethsaida, while he sent the people home. [46]Afterward he went up into the hills by himself to pray.

[47]During the night, the disciples were in their boat out in the middle of the lake, and Jesus was alone on land. [48]He saw that they were in serious trouble, rowing hard and struggling

6:37 Greek *200 denarii*. A denarius was the equivalent of a full day's wage.

unexpected

VENTURING OUT

Our culture values strategy and planning. We do this primarily to make life easier and avoid potential problems. Yet if you look at Jesus in the Gospels, you don't see him taking a poll on where to find a receptive audience and then directing all his ministry efforts there. In fact, we often find him launching out into uncharted waters—boldly willing to encounter only God-knows-what.

In Mark 5 we see him deliberately crossing the Sea of Galilee to encounter a lot of Gentiles. The results are mixed. Some embrace him and his message. Others plead with him to go away.

How willing are *we* to venture outside our comfort zones? What governs our behavior—the will of God or the fear of potential trouble?

MARK 5:1-17

against the wind and waves. About three o'clock in the morning* he came to them, walking on the water. He started to go past them, ⁴⁹but when they saw him walking on the water, they screamed in terror, thinking he was a ghost. ⁵⁰They were all terrified when they saw him. But Jesus spoke to them at once. "It's all right," he said. "I am here! Don't be afraid." ⁵¹Then he climbed into the boat, and the wind stopped. They were astonished at what they saw. ⁵²They still didn't understand the significance of the miracle of the multiplied loaves, for their hearts were hard and they did not believe.

⁵³When they arrived at Gennesaret on the other side of the lake, they anchored the boat ⁵⁴and climbed out. The people standing there recognized him at once, ⁵⁵and they ran throughout the whole area and began carrying sick people to him on mats. ⁵⁶Wherever he went—in villages and cities and out on the farms—they laid the sick in the market plazas and streets. The sick begged him to let them at least touch the fringe of his robe, and all who touched it were healed.

7 Jesus Teaches about Inner Purity

One day some Pharisees and teachers of religious law arrived from Jerusalem to confront Jesus. ²They noticed that some of Jesus' disciples failed to follow the usual Jewish ritual of hand washing before eating. ³(The Jews, especially the Pharisees, do not eat until they have poured water over their cupped hands,* as required by their ancient traditions. ⁴Similarly, they eat nothing bought from the market unless they have immersed their hands in water. This is but one of many traditions they have clung to—such as their ceremony of washing cups, pitchers, and kettles.*) ⁵So the Pharisees and teachers of religious law asked him, "Why don't your disciples follow our age-old customs? For they eat without first performing the hand-washing ceremony."

Buffet

Jesus is teaching an enormous crowd in the middle of nowhere. After a while, the disciples approach Jesus and notify him of the time (it's *meal*time, and stomachs are growling). Jesus looks at his disciples, then at the masses, smiles, and says, "Well, why don't you give them something to eat?"

The disciples panic. They are in a remote place—no Matzo Hut, no Bagel King, nothing. So, they locate a boy's meager sack lunch and bring it to Jesus. Jesus promptly turns that snack into an all-you-can-eat fish and bread buffet for the crowd of perhaps ten thousand people (counting women and children).

Jesus was testing his disciples' faith. He wanted to show them how much he could do with next-to-nothing.

When your resources are nearing empty, do what you can. Then ask God to do the rest.

MARK 6:35-44

Xtraordinary
BUT TRUE

6:48 Greek *About the fourth watch of the night.* 7:3 Greek *washed with the fist.* 7:4 Some Greek manuscripts add *and dining couches.*

[6]Jesus replied, "You hypocrites! Isaiah was prophesying about you when he said,

[7] 'These people honor me with their lips,
    but their hearts are far away.
Their worship is a farce,
    for they replace God's commands with
        their own man-made teachings.'*

[8]For you ignore God's specific laws and substitute your own traditions."

[9]Then he said, "You reject God's laws in order to hold on to your own traditions. [10]For instance, Moses gave you this law from God: 'Honor your father and mother,' and 'Anyone who speaks evil of father or mother must be put to death.'* [11]But you say it is all right for people to say to their parents, 'Sorry, I can't help you. For I have vowed to give to God what I could have given to you.'* [12]You let them disregard their needy parents. [13]As such, you break the law of God in order to protect your own tradition. And this is only one example. There are many, many others."

[14]Then Jesus called to the crowd to come and hear. "All of you listen," he said, "and try to understand. [15]You are not defiled by what you eat; you are defiled by what you say and do!*"

[17]Then Jesus went into a house to get away

A single thought can lead to evil. Don't let sin get a grip in your mind. (7:21-23)

from the crowds, and his disciples asked him what he meant by the statement he had made. [18]"Don't you understand either?" he asked. "Can't you see that what you eat won't defile you? [19]Food doesn't come in contact with your heart, but only passes through the stomach and then comes out again." (By saying this, he showed that every kind of food is acceptable.)

[20]And then he added, "It is the thought-life that defiles you. [21]For from within, out of a person's heart, come evil thoughts, sexual immorality, theft, murder, [22]adultery, greed, wickedness, deceit, eagerness for lustful pleasure, envy, slander, pride, and foolishness. [23]All these vile things come from within; they are what defile you and make you unacceptable to God."

The Faith of a Gentile Woman

[24]Then Jesus left Galilee and went north to the region of Tyre.* He tried to keep it secret that he was there, but he couldn't. As usual, the

7:7 Isa 29:13. **7:10** Exod 20:12; 21:17; Lev 20:9; Deut 5:16. **7:11** Greek *'What I could have given to you is Corban' (that is, a gift).* **7:15** Some manuscripts add verse 16, *Anyone who is willing to hear should listen and understand.* **7:24** Some Greek manuscripts add *and Sidon.*

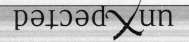

unexpected

GETAWAY

If you've only got three years to accomplish a huge, important mission, common sense would seem to call for getting *busy*, getting *going*.

Instead, Mark 6 finds Jesus and his followers getting *away*—away from the crowds and away from the pressure and stress.

This principle is very important. God built a work-rest rhythm into the fabric of life. When we press too hard and fail to make time for "R & R," we risk burning out.

Leave it to Jesus to teach us something profound about leisure!

MARK 6:31

news of his arrival spread fast. ²⁵Right away a woman came to him whose little girl was possessed by an evil spirit. She had heard about Jesus, and now she came and fell at his feet. ²⁶She begged him to release her child from the demon's control.

Since she was a Gentile, born in Syrian Phoenicia, ²⁷Jesus told her, "First I should help my own family, the Jews.* It isn't right to take food from the children and throw it to the dogs."

²⁸She replied, "That's true, Lord, but even the dogs under the table are given some crumbs from the children's plates."

²⁹"Good answer!" he said. "And because you have answered so well, I have healed your daughter." ³⁰And when she arrived home, her little girl was lying quietly in bed, and the demon was gone.

Jesus Heals a Deaf and Mute Man

³¹Jesus left Tyre and went to Sidon, then back to the Sea of Galilee and the region of the Ten Towns.* ³²A deaf man with a speech impediment was brought to him, and the people begged Jesus to lay his hands on the man to heal him. ³³Jesus led him to a private place away from the crowd. He put his fingers into the man's ears. Then, spitting onto his own fingers, he touched the man's tongue with the spittle. ³⁴And looking up to heaven, he sighed and commanded, "Be opened!"* ³⁵Instantly the man could hear perfectly and speak plainly!

³⁶Jesus told the crowd not to tell anyone, but the more he told them not to, the more they spread the news, ³⁷for they were completely amazed.

Again and again they said, "Everything he does is wonderful. He even heals those who are deaf and mute."

8

Jesus Feeds Four Thousand

About this time another great crowd had gathered, and the people ran out of food again. Jesus called his disciples and told them, ²"I feel sorry for these people. They have been here with me for three days, and they have nothing left to eat. ³And if I send them home without feeding

Dog Lady

Did you know Jesus once called a woman a dog? He did—in a roundabout sort of way. But it wasn't like it sounds.

A Gentile woman with a sick daughter sought out Jesus hoping to find a cure. She knew she would probably be turned away since she wasn't Jewish, but she was desperate, so she came anyway.

In making a reference to "giving food to dogs" Jesus wasn't being derogatory. He was citing his God-given priority to reach Israel first, then the rest of the world. And he was acknowledging the fact that most Jews considered themselves better than non-Jews.

Nevertheless, the lady's faith moved Jesus. Even though she didn't have any of the spiritual advantages the Jewish people did, she recognized who Jesus was, and is.

MARK 7:28

Xtraordinary BUT TRUE

7:27 Greek *Let the children eat first.* 7:31 Greek *Decapolis.* 7:34 Greek text uses Aramaic *"Ephphatha"* and then translates it as "Be opened."

Jesus cares for the total person. He knows your physical needs as well as your spiritual ones. (8:2)

them, they will faint along the road. For some of them have come a long distance."

⁴"How are we supposed to find enough food for them here in the wilderness?" his disciples asked.

⁵"How many loaves of bread do you have?" he asked.

"Seven," they replied. ⁶So Jesus told all the people to sit down on the ground. Then he took the seven loaves, thanked God for them, broke them into pieces, and gave them to his disciples, who distributed the bread to the crowd. ⁷A few small fish were found, too, so Jesus also blessed these and told the disciples to pass them out.

⁸They ate until they were full, and when the scraps were picked up, there were seven large baskets of food left over! ⁹There were about four thousand people in the crowd that day, and he sent them home after they had eaten. ¹⁰Immediately after this, he got into a boat with his disciples and crossed over to the region of Dalmanutha.

Pharisees Demand a Miraculous Sign

¹¹When the Pharisees heard that Jesus had arrived, they came to argue with him. Testing him to see if he was from God, they demanded, "Give us a miraculous sign from heaven to prove yourself."

¹²When he heard this, he sighed deeply and said, "Why do you people keep demanding a miraculous sign? I assure you, I will not give this generation any such sign." ¹³So he got back into the boat and left them, and he crossed to the other side of the lake.

Yeast of the Pharisees and Herod

¹⁴But the disciples discovered they had forgotten to bring any food, so there was only one loaf of bread with them in the boat. ¹⁵As they were crossing the lake, Jesus warned them, "Beware of the yeast of the Pharisees and of Herod."

¹⁶They decided he was saying this because they hadn't brought any bread. ¹⁷Jesus knew what they were thinking, so he said, "Why are you so worried about having no food? Won't you ever learn or understand? Are your hearts

unXpected

RULES

God *must* love rules, right? After all he's the one who came up with the original Top Ten list (the Ten Commandments). And any Bible reader knows that Exodus and Leviticus contain hundreds of other statutes and decrees.

Along come the Pharisees, who take rule-keeping to the ultimate level. They are scrupulous. Meticulous. Obsessed.

Then comes Jesus. Surely he will praise the Pharisees' religious devotion, right? Wrong! He chews them up one side and down the other! They weren't trying to obey God and serve others out of love. They were trying to impress others out of pride!

God hated such hypocrisy then, and he still hates it today!

MARK 7:5-7

too hard to take it in? ¹⁸'You have eyes—can't you see? You have ears—can't you hear?'* Don't you remember anything at all? ¹⁹What about the five thousand men I fed with five loaves of bread? How many baskets of leftovers did you pick up afterward?"

"Twelve," they said.

²⁰"And when I fed the four thousand with seven loaves, how many large baskets of leftovers did you pick up?"

"Seven," they said.

²¹"Don't you understand even yet?" he asked them.

Jesus Heals a Blind Man

²²When they arrived at Bethsaida, some people brought a blind man to Jesus, and they begged him to touch and heal the man. ²³Jesus took the blind man by the hand and led him out of the village. Then, spitting on the man's eyes, he laid his hands on him and asked, "Can you see anything now?"

²⁴The man looked around. "Yes," he said, "I see people, but I can't see them very clearly. They look like trees walking around."

²⁵Then Jesus placed his hands over the man's eyes again. As the man stared intently, his sight was completely restored, and he could see everything clearly. ²⁶Jesus sent him home, saying, "Don't go back into the village on your way home."

Peter's Declaration about Jesus

²⁷Jesus and his disciples left Galilee and went up to the villages of Caesarea Philippi. As they were walking along, he asked them, "Who do people say I am?"

²⁸"Well," they replied, "some say John the Baptist, some say Elijah, and others say you are one of the other prophets."

²⁹Then Jesus asked, "Who do you say I am?"

Peter replied, "You are the Messiah." ³⁰But Jesus warned them not to tell anyone about him.

Jesus Predicts His Death

³¹Then Jesus began to tell them that he, the Son of Man, would suffer many terrible things and be rejected by the leaders, the leading priests, and the teachers of religious law. He would be killed, and three days later he would rise again. ³²As he talked about this openly with his disciples, Peter took him aside and told him he shouldn't say things like that.*

³³Jesus turned and looked at his disciples and then said to Peter very sternly, "Get away from me, Satan! You are seeing things merely from a human point of view, not from God's."

Here's Spit in Your Eye!

Spit is, well, gross. Even your own saliva is nasty, much less someone else's.

So imagine the shock when Jesus healed a deaf man with a speech impediment using *spit*. He didn't have to—he could have simply spoken a word or touched the man. Instead, he spit on his own finger and rubbed it on the man's tongue. Disgusting, huh?

But not to the man who went away jabbering excitedly like a crazy fool—talking for the first time in his life!

Just about the time we think we have Jesus figured out, he does something new and extraordinary to accomplish his will.

MARK 7:33

Xtraordinary
BUT TRUE

8:18 Jer 5:21. 8:32 Or *and began to correct him.*

[34]Then he called his disciples and the crowds to come over and listen. "If any of you wants to be my follower," he told them, "you must put aside your selfish ambition, shoulder your cross, and follow me. [35]If you try to keep your life for yourself, you will lose it. But if you give up your life for my sake and for the sake of the Good News, you will find true life. [36]And how do you benefit if you gain the whole world but lose your own soul* in the process? [37]Is anything worth more than your soul? [38]If a person is ashamed of me and my message in these adulterous and sinful days, I, the Son of Man, will be ashamed of that person when I return in the glory of my Father with the holy angels."

9 Jesus went on to say, "I assure you that some of you standing here right now will not die before you see the Kingdom of God arrive in great power!"

The Transfiguration

[2]Six days later Jesus took Peter, James, and John to the top of a mountain. No one else was there. As the men watched, Jesus' appearance changed, [3]and his clothing became dazzling white, far whiter than any earthly

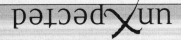

shouLdering the cross means more than wearing one around your neck. It means dying to your desires and Living for God. (8:34)

process could ever make it. [4]Then Elijah and Moses appeared and began talking with Jesus.

[5]"Teacher, this is wonderful!" Peter exclaimed. "We will make three shrines*—one for you, one for Moses, and one for Elijah." [6]He didn't really know what to say, for they were all terribly afraid.

[7]Then a cloud came over them, and a voice from the cloud said, "This is my beloved Son. Listen to him." [8]Suddenly they looked around, and Moses and Elijah were gone, and only Jesus was with them. [9]As they descended the mountainside, he told them not to tell anyone what they had seen until he, the Son of Man, had risen from the dead. [10]So they kept it to themselves, but they often asked each other what he meant by "rising from the dead."

[11]Now they began asking him, "Why do the

8:36 Or *your life;* also in 8:37. **9:5** Or *shelters;* Greek reads *tabernacles.*

---

uneXpected

SPECIAL EFFECTS

The visual effects in the newest sci-fi movie are spectacular. But when you see a TV special about how the creators used computer animation, models, and trick photography, it's not quite so impressive.

Rewind now to the historic moment of the Transfiguration. For a few brief moments on a mountaintop, Jesus' divine nature was revealed to Peter, James, and John. He positively glowed with the brilliant glory and pure radiance of deity. Elijah and Moses showed up! God spoke *audibly*!

It was a truly awesome, *real-life* event, not a Hollywood special effect. And the point was to show that the humble teacher from Nazareth is far superior to Israel's greatest leaders. He is, in fact, God!

MARK 9:2-9

SON OF GOD

Mark's gospel was written for a Roman audience, primarily for Gentiles rather than Jews. Mark wrote to portray Christ as the suffering servant who came to give his life "as a ransom for many" (Mark 10:45). The power and authority of his service and sacrifice comes from the fact that he *was* (and is) God. Therefore, Mark brackets his Gospel with the use of the name "Son of God" to introduce his readers to Jesus (Mark 1:1) and near the end of the book with the Roman officer's exclamation at the cross, "Truly, this was the Son of God" (Mark 15:39).

Do you recognize Jesus as the Son of God?

Xalt Him!

teachers of religious law insist that Elijah must return before the Messiah comes?"

12Jesus responded, "Elijah is indeed coming first to set everything in order. Why then is it written in the Scriptures that the Son of Man must suffer and be treated with utter contempt? 13But I tell you, Elijah has already come, and he was badly mistreated, just as the Scriptures predicted."

Jesus Heals a Boy Possessed by an Evil Spirit
14At the foot of the mountain they found a great crowd surrounding the other disciples, as some teachers of religious law were arguing with them. 15The crowd watched Jesus in awe as he came toward them, and then they ran to greet him. 16"What is all this arguing about?" he asked.

17One of the men in the crowd spoke up and said, "Teacher, I brought my son for you to heal him. He can't speak because he is possessed by an evil spirit that won't let him talk. 18And whenever this evil spirit seizes him, it throws him violently to the ground and makes him foam at the mouth and grind his teeth and become rigid.* So I asked your dis-

9:18 Or *become weak.*   9:29 Some manuscripts add *and fasting.*

ciples to cast out the evil spirit, but they couldn't do it."

19Jesus said to them, "You faithless people! How long must I be with you until you believe? How long must I put up with you? Bring the boy to me." 20So they brought the boy. But when the evil spirit saw Jesus, it threw the child into a violent convulsion, and he fell to the ground, writhing and foaming at the mouth. 21"How long has this been happening?" Jesus asked the boy's father.

He replied, "Since he was very small. 22The evil spirit often makes him fall into the fire or into water, trying to kill him. Have mercy on us and help us. Do something if you can."

23"What do you mean, 'If I can'?" Jesus asked. "Anything is possible if a person believes."

24The father instantly replied, "I do believe, but help me not to doubt!"

25When Jesus saw that the crowd of onlookers was growing, he rebuked the evil spirit. "Spirit of deafness and muteness," he said, "I command you to come out of this child and never enter him again!" 26Then the spirit screamed and threw the boy into another violent convulsion and left him. The boy lay there motionless, and he appeared to be dead. A murmur ran through the crowd, "He's dead." 27But Jesus took him by the hand and helped him to his feet, and he stood up.

28Afterward, when Jesus was alone in the house with his disciples, they asked him, "Why couldn't we cast out that evil spirit?"

29Jesus replied, "This kind can be cast out only by prayer.*"

Jesus Again Predicts His Death
30Leaving that region, they traveled through Galilee. Jesus tried to avoid all publicity 31in order to spend more time with his disciples and teach them. He said to them, "The Son of Man is going to be betrayed. He will be killed,

Got doubts? Ask God to give you the faith to trust him.

(9:24)

HeLping out a stranger is Like heLping out Jesus instead. (9:41)

but three days later he will rise from the dead." [32]But they didn't understand what he was saying, and they were afraid to ask him what he meant.

The Greatest in the Kingdom
[33]After they arrived at Capernaum, Jesus and his disciples settled in the house where they would be staying. Jesus asked them, "What were you discussing out on the road?" [34]But they didn't answer, because they had been arguing about which of them was the greatest. [35]He sat down and called the twelve disciples over to him. Then he said, "Anyone who wants to be the first must take last place and be the servant of everyone else."

[36]Then he put a little child among them. Taking the child in his arms, he said to them, [37]"Anyone who welcomes a little child like this on my behalf welcomes me, and anyone who welcomes me welcomes my Father who sent me."

Using the Name of Jesus
[38]John said to Jesus, "Teacher, we saw a man using your name to cast out demons, but we told him to stop because he isn't one of our group."

[39]"Don't stop him!" Jesus said. "No one who performs miracles in my name will soon be able to speak evil of me. [40]Anyone who is not against us is for us. [41]If anyone gives you even a cup of water because you belong to the Messiah, I assure you, that person will be rewarded.

[42]"But if anyone causes one of these little ones who trusts in me to lose faith, it would be better for that person to be thrown into the sea with a large millstone tied around the neck. [43]If your hand causes you to sin, cut it off. It is better to enter heaven* with only one hand than to go into the unquenchable fires of hell with two hands.* [45]If your foot causes you to sin, cut it off. It is better to enter heaven with only one foot than to be thrown into hell with two feet.* [47]And if your eye causes you to sin,

9:43a Greek *enter life;* also in 9:45. 9:43b Some manuscripts add verse 44 (which is identical with 9:48). 9:45 Some manuscripts add verse 46 (which is identical with 9:48).

un**X**pected

KIDS WELCOME!

In a society that firmly believed the old adage "Children should be seen and not heard," Jesus caused quite a commotion.

He once plucked a little kid out of the crowd and hugged him to his chest. Then he basically told everyone listening that if you want to be great in heaven's eyes, and if you truly love God, you'll treat people well—even little people, *especially* little people.

The point, of course, is that everyone matters to God, and we are sadly mistaken if we think God views one group of folks as more important than another.

How do *you* treat younger kids? Older folks? People of different ethnic backgrounds?

MARK 9:37

Splitsville

I don't understand how people can just stop loving each other. Especially after twenty years of marriage! I also don't understand how none of us kids could see it coming. As far as we knew, Mom and Dad loved each other, and we were the perfect family. Now it feels like it was all just one big show, like Mom and Dad were lying to us the whole time.

So the one thing in my life that I thought was stable turns out to be this big joke, something that can be thrown away like trash. That really hurts.

On top of that, suddenly I feel like I have to be a parent for my little brother and sister. Hey, somebody has to do it. If my mom and dad can stop loving each other, I feel like they can stop loving us, too. We can't handle going through that kind of pain again. Maybe I'm overreacting a little, but that's how I feel.

Mom and Dad act like they're doing us a favor by letting us choose who we want to live with. Like we should be happy that we have a say in something. It's like, "Hey, you can't do anything about us ruining your life, but we'll let you choose whose house you want to be miserable in." Thanks a lot.

Now I understand why the Bible says God hates divorce. I think it's because he knows what it does to kids, and he doesn't want them to have to go through this kind of pain. It's just too bad that parents don't feel the same way about it.

At least I don't ever have to worry about God walking out on me. When he says, "I'll be with you forever," he really means it.

Alec

READ IT IN MARK 10:1-9.

real Xpressions

gouge it out. It is better to enter the Kingdom of God half blind than to have two eyes and be thrown into hell, 48'where the worm never dies and the fire never goes out.'*

49"For everyone will be purified with fire.* 50Salt is good for seasoning. But if it loses its flavor, how do you make it salty again? You must have the qualities of salt among yourselves and live in peace with each other."

10 Discussion about Divorce and Marriage

Then Jesus left Capernaum and went southward to the region of Judea and into the area east of the Jordan River. As always there were the crowds, and as usual he taught them.

2Some Pharisees came and tried to trap him with this question: "Should a man be allowed to divorce his wife?"

3"What did Moses say about divorce?" Jesus asked them.

4"Well, he permitted it," they replied. "He said a man merely has to write his wife an official letter of divorce and send her away."*

5But Jesus responded, "He wrote those instructions only as a concession to your hardhearted wickedness. 6But God's plan was seen from the beginning of creation, for 'He made them male and female.'* 7'This explains why a man leaves his father and mother and is joined to his wife,* 8and the two are united into one.'* Since they are no longer two but one, 9let no one separate them, for God has joined them together."

10Later, when he was alone with his disci-

9:48 Isa 66:24. 9:49 Greek salted with fire. Some manuscripts add and every sacrifice will be salted with salt. 10:4 Deut 24:1. 10:6 Gen 1:27; 5:2. 10:7 Some manuscripts do not include and is joined to his wife. 10:7-8 Gen 2:24.

ples in the house, they brought up the subject again. ¹¹He told them, "Whoever divorces his wife and marries someone else commits adultery against her. ¹²And if a woman divorces her husband and remarries, she commits adultery."

Jesus Blesses the Children
¹³One day some parents brought their children to Jesus so he could touch them and bless them, but the disciples told them not to bother him. ¹⁴But when Jesus saw what was happening, he was very displeased with his disciples. He said to them, "Let the children come to me. Don't stop them! For the Kingdom of God belongs to such as these. ¹⁵I assure you, anyone who doesn't have their kind of faith will never get into the Kingdom of God." ¹⁶Then he took the children into his arms and placed his hands on their heads and blessed them.

The Rich Man
¹⁷As he was starting out on a trip, a man came running up to Jesus, knelt down, and asked, "Good Teacher, what should I do to get eternal life?"

¹⁸"Why do you call me good?" Jesus asked. "Only God is truly good. ¹⁹But as for your question, you know the commandments: 'Do not murder. Do not commit adultery. Do not

Money can buy you a lot of stuff, but it can't buy your way into heaven. Jesus is the only ticket. (10:25)

steal. Do not testify falsely. Do not cheat. Honor your father and mother.'*"

²⁰"Teacher," the man replied, "I've obeyed all these commandments since I was a child."

²¹Jesus felt genuine love for this man as he looked at him. "You lack only one thing," he told him. "Go and sell all you have and give the money to the poor, and you will have treasure in heaven. Then come, follow me." ²²At this, the man's face fell, and he went sadly away because he had many possessions.

²³Jesus looked around and said to his disciples, "How hard it is for rich people to get into the Kingdom of God!" ²⁴This amazed them. But Jesus said again, "Dear children, it is very hard* to get into the Kingdom of God. ²⁵It is easier for a camel to go through the eye of a needle than for a rich person to enter the Kingdom of God!"

²⁶The disciples were astounded. "Then who in the world can be saved?" they asked.

10:19 Exod 20:12-16; Deut 5:16-20. **10:24** Some manuscripts add *for those who trust in riches.*

unXpected

KID STUFF

Many adults tend to view faith in God as something that requires deep intellect and keen powers of reasoning. Maybe this is why, in a lot of churches, little kids are shuttled off to "junior church" to color and watch puppets while the older folks stay in "big church" and talk about "deep doctrinal issues."

Yet if you listen to Jesus, he describes faith using *children* as role models. The Gospels repeatedly picture Jesus as a Savior who seemed drawn to kids. Perhaps this was because they are not so hung up in trying to understand all mysteries. Or maybe because they are more willing to trust.

We can and should grow in our *understanding* of the faith, but nothing beats *having* faith that is as accepting and trusting as that of a child.

MARK 10:14

Jesus' mission was straight-forward: Give up his Life on earth so others might Live forever. (10:45)

[27]Jesus looked at them intently and said, "Humanly speaking, it is impossible. But not with God. Everything is possible with God."

[28]Then Peter began to mention all that he and the other disciples had left behind. "We've given up everything to follow you," he said.

[29]And Jesus replied, "I assure you that everyone who has given up house or brothers or sisters or mother or father or children or property, for my sake and for the Good News, [30]will receive now in return, a hundred times over, houses, brothers, sisters, mothers, children, and property—with persecutions. And in the world to come they will have eternal life. [31]But many who seem to be important now will be the least important then, and those who are considered least here will be the greatest then.*"

Jesus Again Predicts His Death
[32]They were now on the way to Jerusalem, and Jesus was walking ahead of them. The disciples were filled with dread and the people following behind were overwhelmed with fear. Taking the twelve disciples aside, Jesus once more began to describe everything that was about to happen to him in Jerusalem. [33]"When we get to Jerusalem," he told them, "the Son of Man will be betrayed to the leading priests and the teachers of religious law. They will sentence him to die and hand him over to the Romans. [34]They will mock him, spit on him, beat him with their whips, and kill him, but after three days he will rise again."

Jesus Teaches about Serving Others
[35]Then James and John, the sons of Zebedee, came over and spoke to him. "Teacher," they said, "we want you to do us a favor."

[36]"What is it?" he asked.

[37]"In your glorious Kingdom, we want to sit in places of honor next to you," they said, "one at your right and the other at your left."

[38]But Jesus answered, "You don't know what you are asking! Are you able to drink from the bitter cup of sorrow I am about to drink? Are you able to be baptized with the baptism of suffering I must be baptized with?"

[39]"Oh yes," they said, "we are able!"

And Jesus said, "You will indeed drink from my cup and be baptized with my baptism, [40]but I have no right to say who will sit on the thrones next to mine. God has prepared those places for the ones he has chosen."

[41]When the ten other disciples discovered what James and John had asked, they were indignant. [42]So Jesus called them together and said, "You know that in this world kings are tyrants, and officials lord it over the people beneath them. [43]But among you it should be quite different. Whoever wants to be a leader among you must be your servant, [44]and whoever wants to be first must be the slave of all. [45]For even I, the Son of Man, came here not to be served but to serve others, and to give my life as a ransom for many."

Jesus Heals Blind Bartimaeus
[46]And so they reached Jericho. Later, as Jesus and his disciples left town, a great crowd was following. A blind beggar named Bartimaeus (son of Timaeus) was sitting beside the road as Jesus was going by. [47]When Bartimaeus heard that Jesus from Nazareth was nearby, he began to shout out, "Jesus, Son of David, have mercy on me!"

[48]"Be quiet!" some of the people yelled at him.

But he only shouted louder, "Son of David, have mercy on me!"

[49]When Jesus heard him, he stopped and said, "Tell him to come here."

So they called the blind man. "Cheer up," they said. "Come on, he's calling you!" [50]Bartimaeus threw aside his coat, jumped up, and came to Jesus.

[51]"What do you want me to do for you?" Jesus asked.

"Teacher," the blind man said, "I want to see!"

[52]And Jesus said to him, "Go your way.

10:31 Greek *But many who are first will be last; and the last, first.*

Your faith has healed you." And instantly the blind man could see! Then he followed Jesus down the road.*

11 The Triumphal Entry

As Jesus and his disciples approached Jerusalem, they came to the towns of Bethphage and Bethany, on the Mount of Olives. Jesus sent two of them on ahead. ²"Go into that village over there," he told them, "and as soon as you enter it, you will see a colt tied there that has never been ridden. Untie it and bring it here. ³If anyone asks what you are doing, just say, 'The Lord needs it and will return it soon.'"

⁴The two disciples left and found the colt standing in the street, tied outside a house. ⁵As they were untying it, some bystanders demanded, "What are you doing, untying that colt?" ⁶They said what Jesus had told them to say, and they were permitted to take it. ⁷Then they brought the colt to Jesus and threw their garments over it, and he sat on it.

⁸Many in the crowd spread their coats on the road ahead of Jesus, and others cut leafy branches in the fields and spread them along the way. ⁹He was in the center of the procession, and the crowds all around him were shouting,

"Praise God!*
  Bless the one who comes in the name
    of the Lord!
¹⁰ Bless the coming kingdom of our ancestor
    David!
  Praise God in highest heaven!"*

¹¹So Jesus came to Jerusalem and went into the Temple. He looked around carefully at everything, and then he left because it was late in the afternoon. Then he went out to Bethany with the twelve disciples.

Jesus Curses the Fig Tree

¹²The next morning as they were leaving Bethany, Jesus felt hungry. ¹³He noticed a fig tree a little way off that was in full leaf, so he went over to see if he could find any figs on it. But there were only leaves because it was too early in the season for fruit. ¹⁴Then Jesus said to the tree, "May no one ever eat your fruit again!" And the disciples heard him say it.

Jesus Clears the Temple

¹⁵When they arrived back in Jerusalem, Jesus entered the Temple and began to drive out the

10:52 Or *on the way.* 11:9 Greek *Hosanna,* an exclamation of praise that literally means "save now"; also in 11:10.
11:9-10 Pss 118:25-26; 148:1.

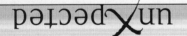

TROUBLEMAKER

Because Bartimaeus was blind, he made a living (such as it was) begging by the roadside. He was little more than an ancient street person. A public nuisance. A human eyesore.

On the day Bartimaeus learned that Jesus was passing by, he got *really* obnoxious. He started yelling. When the crowd (including a few of Christ's followers) told him to shut up, Bartimaeus only screamed louder.

Jesus eventually stopped and called the desperate man to himself. Stumbling through the mob, Bartimaeus made his way to Christ and received physical and spiritual healing. Then he, too, became a follower of Jesus.

This unexpected story prompts the question: What "undesirables" in your life need the touch of Christ today?

MARK 10:46-52

merchants and their customers. He knocked over the tables of the money changers and the stalls of those selling doves, [16]and he stopped everyone from bringing in merchandise. [17]He taught them, "The Scriptures declare, 'My Temple will be called a place of prayer for all nations,' but you have turned it into a den of thieves."*

[18]When the leading priests and teachers of religious law heard what Jesus had done, they began planning how to kill him. But they were afraid of him because the people were so enthusiastic about Jesus' teaching. [19]That evening Jesus and the disciples* left the city.

[20]The next morning as they passed by the fig tree he had cursed, the disciples noticed it was withered from the roots. [21]Peter remembered what Jesus had said to the tree on the previous day and exclaimed, "Look, Teacher! The fig tree you cursed has withered!"

[22]Then Jesus said to the disciples, "Have faith in God. [23]I assure you that you can say to this mountain, 'May God lift you up and throw you into the sea,' and your command will be obeyed. All that's required is that you really believe and do not doubt in your heart. [24]Listen to me! You can pray for anything, and if you believe, you will have it. [25]But when you are praying, first forgive anyone you are holding a grudge against, so that your Father in heaven will forgive your sins, too.*"

The Authority of Jesus Challenged

[27]By this time they had arrived in Jerusalem again. As Jesus was walking through the Temple area, the leading priests, the teachers of religious law, and the other leaders came up to him. They demanded, [28]"By whose authority did you drive out the merchants from the Temple?* Who gave you such authority?"

[29]"I'll tell who gave me authority to do these things if you answer one question," Jesus replied. [30]"Did John's baptism come from heaven or was it merely human? Answer me!"

[31]They talked it over among themselves. "If we say it was from heaven, he will ask why we didn't believe him. [32]But do we dare say it was merely human?" For they were afraid that the people would start a riot, since everyone thought that John was a prophet. [33]So they finally replied, "We don't know."

Horse Thief?

Whoever said the Bible is dull must have missed all the wild, fascinating stories like this one! Imagine Jesus telling two of your friends, "Go out into the suburbs where you'll see a Chevy dealership. There on the lot, you'll find a brand-new Corvette. Get in it and drive it back here to me. If a salesman stops you, just say, 'The Lord needs it.'"

Yeah, right! Try that and see how far it gets you—most likely 5 to 10 in the state pen!

Yet that's essentially what Jesus instructed two of his disciples to do (only with a donkey's colt—not a sports car!). And everything worked out just as Jesus said—because this was all part of God's prophetic plan (see Zechariah 9:9).

MARK 11:2-3

Xtraordinary
BUT TRUE

11:17 Isa 56:7; Jer 7:11. **11:19** Greek *they;* some manuscripts read *he.* **11:25** Some manuscripts add verse 26, *But if you do not forgive, neither will your Father who is in heaven forgive your sins.* **11:28** Or *By whose authority do you do these things?*

And Jesus responded, "Then I won't answer your question either."

12

Story of the Evil Farmers

Then Jesus began telling them stories: "A man planted a vineyard, built a wall around it, dug a pit for pressing out the grape juice, and built a lookout tower. Then he leased the vineyard to tenant farmers and moved to another country. ²At grape-picking time he sent one of his servants to collect his share of the crop. ³But the farmers grabbed the servant, beat him up, and sent him back empty-handed.

⁴"The owner then sent another servant, but they beat him over the head and treated him shamefully. ⁵The next servant he sent was killed. Others who were sent were either beaten or killed, ⁶until there was only one left—his son whom he loved dearly. The owner finally sent him, thinking, 'Surely they will respect my son.'

⁷"But the farmers said to one another, 'Here comes the heir to this estate. Let's kill him and get the estate for ourselves!' ⁸So they grabbed him and murdered him and threw his body out of the vineyard.

12:10-11 Ps 118:22-23.

⁹"What do you suppose the owner of the vineyard will do?" Jesus asked. "I'll tell you—he will come and kill them all and lease the vineyard to others. ¹⁰Didn't you ever read this in the Scriptures?

'The stone rejected by the builders
    has now become the cornerstone.
¹¹This is the Lord's doing,
    and it is marvelous to see.'*"

¹²The Jewish leaders wanted to arrest him for using this illustration because they realized he was pointing at them—they were the wicked farmers in his story. But they were afraid to touch him because of the crowds. So they left him and went away.

Taxes for Caesar

¹³The leaders sent some Pharisees and supporters of Herod to try to trap Jesus into saying something for which he could be arrested. ¹⁴"Teacher," these men said, "we know how honest you are. You are impartial and don't play favorites. You sincerely teach the ways of God. Now tell us—is it right to pay taxes to the Roman government or not? ¹⁵Should we pay them, or should we not?"

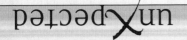

unexpected

MEASURED WORDS

Marriage counselors often give warring couples communication advice like: "Avoid inflammatory language. Choose your words carefully. Try not to push each other's buttons."

This is all good counsel that can help us steer clear of needless conflict. But sometimes conflict is unavoidable. Sometimes the truth must be stated clearly and without mincing words.

Mark 12 begins with Jesus telling a pointed parable aimed right at the Pharisees. He didn't back away from portraying them in an unflattering light. And they responded as we would expect—with outrage and a renewed determination to silence Jesus.

How willing are you to say hard things to others if a situation calls for such action?

MARK 12:12

Jesus saw through their hypocrisy and said, "Whom are you trying to fool with your trick questions? Show me a Roman coin,* and I'll tell you." 16When they handed it to him, he asked, "Whose picture and title are stamped on it?"

"Caesar's," they replied.

17"Well, then," Jesus said, "give to Caesar what belongs to him. But everything that belongs to God must be given to God." This reply completely amazed them.

Discussion about Resurrection

18Then the Sadducees stepped forward— a group of Jews who say there is no resurrection after death. They posed this question: 19"Teacher, Moses gave us a law that if a man dies, leaving a wife without children, his brother should marry the widow and have a child who will be the brother's heir.* 20Well, there were seven brothers. The oldest of them married and then died without children. 21So the second brother married the widow, but soon he too died and left no children. Then the next brother married her and died without children. 22This continued until all the brothers had married her and died, and still there were no children. Last of all, the woman died, too. 23So tell us, whose wife will she be in the resurrection? For all seven were married to her."

Respect earthly authorities, but give God your total allegiance. (12:17)

24Jesus replied, "Your problem is that you don't know the Scriptures, and you don't know the power of God. 25For when the dead rise, they won't be married. They will be like the angels in heaven. 26But now, as to whether the dead will be raised—haven't you ever read about this in the writings of Moses, in the story of the burning bush? Long after Abraham, Isaac, and Jacob had died, God said to Moses,* 'I am the God of Abraham, the God of Isaac, and the God of Jacob.'* 27So he is the

Can you summarize the entire Bible in two sentences? Jesus did. Love God. Love others. (12:30-31)

God of the living, not the dead. You have made a serious error."

The Most Important Commandment

28One of the teachers of religious law was standing there listening to the discussion. He realized that Jesus had answered well, so he asked, "Of all the commandments, which is the most important?"

29Jesus replied, "The most important commandment is this: 'Hear, O Israel! The Lord our God is the one and only Lord. 30And you must love the Lord your God with all your heart, all your soul, all your mind, and all your strength.'* 31The second is equally important: 'Love your neighbor as yourself.'* No other commandment is greater than these."

32The teacher of religious law replied, "Well said, Teacher. You have spoken the truth by saying that there is only one God and no other. 33And I know it is important to love him with all my heart and all my understanding and all my strength, and to love my neighbors as myself. This is more important than to offer all of the burnt offerings and sacrifices required in the law."

34Realizing this man's understanding, Jesus said to him, "You are not far from the Kingdom of God." And after that, no one dared to ask him any more questions.

Whose Son Is the Messiah?

35Later, as Jesus was teaching the people in the Temple, he asked, "Why do the teachers of religious law claim that the Messiah will be the son of David? 36For David himself, speaking under the inspiration of the Holy Spirit, said,

'The LORD said to my Lord,
Sit in honor at my right hand
   until I humble your enemies beneath
      your feet.'*

12:15 Greek *a denarius*. 12:19 Deut 25:5-6. 12:26a Greek *in the story of the bush? God said to him*. 12:26b Exod 3:6. 12:29-30 Deut 6:4-5. 12:31 Lev 19:18. 12:36 Ps 110:1.

³⁷Since David himself called him Lord, how can he be his son at the same time?" And the crowd listened to him with great interest.

³⁸Here are some of the other things he taught them at this time: "Beware of these teachers of religious law! For they love to parade in flowing robes and to have everyone bow to them as they walk in the marketplaces. ³⁹And how they love the seats of honor in the synagogues and at banquets. ⁴⁰But they shamelessly cheat widows out of their property, and then, to cover up the kind of people they really are, they make long prayers in public. Because of this, their punishment will be the greater."

The Widow's Offering

⁴¹Jesus went over to the collection box in the Temple and sat and watched as the crowds dropped in their money. Many rich people put in large amounts. ⁴²Then a poor widow came and dropped in two pennies.* ⁴³He called his disciples to him and said, "I assure you, this poor widow has given more than all the others have given. ⁴⁴For they gave a tiny part of their surplus, but she, poor as she is, has given everything she has."

12:42 Greek *2 lepta, which is a kodrantes.* 13:6 Greek *name, saying, 'I am.'*

13

Jesus Foretells the Future

As Jesus was leaving the Temple that day, one of his disciples said, "Teacher, look at these tremendous buildings! Look at the massive stones in the walls!"

²Jesus replied, "These magnificent buildings will be so completely demolished that not one stone will be left on top of another."

³Later, Jesus sat on the slopes of the Mount of Olives across the valley from the Temple. Peter, James, John, and Andrew came to him privately and asked him, ⁴"When will all this take place? And will there be any sign ahead of time to show us when all this will be fulfilled?"

⁵Jesus replied, "Don't let anyone mislead you, ⁶because many will come in my name, claiming to be the Messiah.* They will lead many astray. ⁷And wars will break out near and far, but don't panic. Yes, these things must come, but the end won't follow immediately. ⁸Nations and kingdoms will proclaim war against each other, and there will be earthquakes in many parts of the world, and famines. But all this will be only the beginning of the horrors to come. ⁹But when these things begin to happen, watch out! You will be

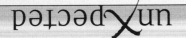

GIVING SACRIFICIALLY

A telethon features an endless line-up of celebrities and business people coming onstage to donate whopping checks: $2.5 million, $500,000, $1.2 million, another for $750,000. This goes on until at last the cameras focus on Mrs. Gladys Smugley from Hazelhurst, Arkansas. She's there to give $12.48—all that's left from her monthly Social Security check.

Suddenly the band starts playing, lights flash, and confetti starts dropping. The host stops the entire show to announce excitedly, "This is our biggest donation yet!"

If you can envision this, you've got a sense of the scene in Mark 12. Jesus' views on giving are totally unexpected—attitude counts far more than amount. Giving merely leftovers—no matter how much—never impresses God.

MARK 12:43-44

handed over to the courts and beaten in the synagogues. You will be accused before governors and kings of being my followers. This will be your opportunity to tell them about me.* 10And the Good News must first be preached to every nation. 11But when you are arrested and stand trial, don't worry about what to say in your defense. Just say what God tells you to. Then it is not you who will be speaking, but the Holy Spirit.

12"Brother will betray brother to death, fathers will betray their own children, and children will rise against their parents and cause them to be killed. 13And everyone will hate you because of your allegiance to me. But those who endure to the end will be saved.

14"The time will come when you will see the sacrilegious object that causes desecration* standing where it should not be"—reader, pay attention! "Then those in Judea must flee to the hills. 15A person outside the house* must not go back into the house to pack. 16A person in the field must not return even to get a coat. 17How terrible it will be for pregnant women and for mothers nursing their babies in those days. 18And pray that your flight will not be in winter. 19For those will be days of greater horror than at any time since God created the world. And it will never happen again. 20In fact, unless the Lord shortens that time of calamity, the entire human race will be destroyed. But for the sake of his chosen ones he has shortened those days.

21"And then if anyone tells you, 'Look, here is the Messiah,' or, 'There he is,' don't pay any attention. 22For false messiahs and false prophets will rise up and perform miraculous signs and wonders so as to deceive, if possible, even God's chosen ones. 23Watch out! I have warned you!

24"At that time, after those horrible days end,

the sun will be darkened,
the moon will not give light,
25 the stars will fall from the sky,
and the powers of heaven will be shaken.*

26Then everyone will see the Son of Man arrive on the clouds with great power and glory.* 27And he will send forth his angels to gather together his chosen ones from all over the world—from the farthest ends of the earth and heaven.

28"Now, learn a lesson from the fig tree. When its buds become tender and its leaves begin to sprout, you know without being told that summer is near. 29Just so, when you see the events I've described beginning to happen, you can be sure that his return is very near, right at the door. 30I assure you, this generation* will not pass from the scene until all these events have taken place. 31Heaven and earth will disappear, but my words will remain forever.

32"However, no one knows the day or hour when these things will happen, not even the angels in heaven or the Son himself. Only the Father knows. 33And since you don't know when they will happen, stay alert and keep watch.*

34"The coming of the Son of Man can be compared with that of a man who left home to go on a trip. He gave each of his employees instructions about the work they were to do, and he told the gatekeeper to watch for his return. 35So keep a sharp lookout! For you do not know when the homeowner will return—at evening, midnight, early dawn, or late daybreak. 36Don't let him find you sleeping when he arrives without warning. 37What I say to you I say to everyone: Watch for his return!"

Keep alert! Stay close to Jesus and his teachings so you won't be led away by lies. (13:22)

14

Jesus Anointed at Bethany
It was now two days before the Passover celebration and the Festival of Unleavened Bread. The leading priests and the teachers of religious law were still

---

13:9 Or *This will be your testimony against them.* **13:14** Greek *the abomination of desolation.* See Dan 9:27; 11:31; 12:11. **13:15** Greek *on the roof.* **13:24-25** See Isa 13:10; 34:4; Joel 2:10. **13:26** See Dan 7:13. **13:30** Or *this age,* or *this nation.* **13:33** Some manuscripts add *and pray.*

looking for an opportunity to capture Jesus secretly and put him to death. 2"But not during the Passover," they agreed, "or there will be a riot."

3Meanwhile, Jesus was in Bethany at the home of Simon, a man who had leprosy. During supper, a woman came in with a beautiful jar of expensive perfume.* She broke the seal and poured the perfume over his head. 4Some of those at the table were indignant. "Why was this expensive perfume wasted?" they asked. 5"She could have sold it for a small fortune* and given the money to the poor!" And they scolded her harshly.

6But Jesus replied, "Leave her alone. Why berate her for doing such a good thing to me? 7You will always have the poor among you, and you can help them whenever you want to. But I will not be here with you much longer. 8She has done what she could and has anointed my body for burial ahead of time. 9I assure you, wherever the Good News is preached throughout the world, this woman's deed will be talked about in her memory."

Judas Agrees to Betray Jesus

10Then Judas Iscariot, one of the twelve disciples, went to the leading priests to arrange to betray Jesus to them. 11The leading priests were delighted when they heard why he had come, and they promised him a reward. So he began looking for the right time and place to betray Jesus.

The Last Supper

12On the first day of the Festival of Unleavened Bread (the day the Passover lambs were sacrificed), Jesus' disciples asked him, "Where do you want us to go to prepare the Passover supper?"

13So Jesus sent two of them into Jerusalem to make the arrangements. "As you go into the city," he told them, "a man carrying a pitcher of water will meet you. Follow him. 14At the house he enters, say to the owner, 'The Teacher asks, Where is the guest room where I can eat the Passover meal with my disciples?' 15He will take you upstairs to a large room that is already set up. That is the place; go ahead and prepare our supper there." 16So the two disciples went on ahead into the city and found everything just as Jesus had said, and they prepared the Passover supper there.

17In the evening Jesus arrived with the twelve disciples. 18As they were sitting around the table eating, Jesus said, "The truth is, one

14:3 Greek *an alabaster jar of expensive ointment, pure nard.* **14:5** Greek *300 denarii.* A denarius was the equivalent of a full day's wage.

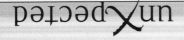

THE BIG SECRET

Jesus kept talking about leaving and coming back, but when the question of "When?" was put to him, he replied that only God knows the exact dates and times for all such future events.

This statement doesn't suggest that Jesus is in the dark, or, worse, that he's not one with God. Rather, it simply means that when the eternal Son of God took on human form, he temporarily laid aside certain divine privileges and powers.

Jesus' point is that we should be prepared to meet God and live in such a way that we're not ashamed when he returns for us (1 John 2:28).

Is this true in your life?

MARK 13:32

Righting a Wrong

For two years—as long as Patty, Tia, and I have played volleyball together—we've been best friends. During that time, I've done everything I can to be a good influence on them. Neither of them are Christians, and I'm trying to change that.

I really believe that God makes himself known in the way Christians talk and act. That's why I've always tried to say and do the right things when I'm around them. Sometimes they tease me about being "Little Miss Perfect," but they also respect me.

At least they did until last Thursday's bus ride.

We were coming home from one of the worst games I've ever played. The coach had been yelling at me all night, and I was completely stressed. By the time we got on the bus, I wasn't in the mood to talk to anyone.

I ended up sitting by myself, across from Patty and Tia. The two girls sitting behind me, whose names I won't mention, started making little comments about players who cost us the game and shouldn't even be allowed on the team.

I tried to ignore them at first, but I just kept getting madder and madder. Finally, I lost it. I turned around and, without even thinking, started saying whatever popped into my head. I don't remember most of the stuff I said, and the parts I do remember I can't repeat. It was that bad.

When I turned back around, Patty was laughing, and Tia had a shocked look on her face. I felt like crying. It was like I'd ruined two years of hard work in two minutes.

So now what? I kept wondering that night. I couldn't avoid my friends and my team. I felt like I knew what I should do, but it wouldn't be easy.

I'll have to apologize to everyone who was on that bus, including Patty and Tia. And then I'm not giving up. Who knows? Maybe God can do something, even with my mistake.

Annie

READ IT IN MARK 14:66-72.

reaL Xpressions

of you will betray me, one of you who is here eating with me."

¹⁹Greatly distressed, one by one they began to ask him, "I'm not the one, am I?"

²⁰He replied, "It is one of you twelve, one who is eating with me now.* ²¹For I, the Son of Man, must die, as the Scriptures declared long ago. But how terrible it will be for my betrayer. Far better for him if he had never been born!"

²²As they were eating, Jesus took a loaf of bread and asked God's blessing on it. Then he broke it in pieces and gave it to the disciples, saying, "Take it, for this is my body."

²³And he took a cup of wine and gave thanks to God for it. He gave it to them, and they all drank from it. ²⁴And he said to them, "This is my blood, poured out for many, sealing the covenant* between God and his people. ²⁵I solemnly declare that I will not drink wine again until that day when I drink it new in the Kingdom of God." ²⁶Then they sang a hymn and went out to the Mount of Olives.

14:20 Or one who is dipping bread into the bowl with me. 14:24 Some manuscripts read the new covenant.

Jesus Predicts Peter's Denial

27"All of you will desert me," Jesus told them. "For the Scriptures say,

> 'God* will strike the Shepherd,
>   and the sheep will be scattered.'*

28But after I am raised from the dead, I will go ahead of you to Galilee and meet you there."

29Peter said to him, "Even if everyone else deserts you, I never will."

30"Peter," Jesus replied, "the truth is, this very night, before the rooster crows twice, you will deny me three times."

31"No!" Peter insisted. "Not even if I have to die with you! I will never deny you!" And all the others vowed the same.

Jesus Prays in Gethsemane

32And they came to an olive grove called Gethsemane, and Jesus said, "Sit here while I go and pray." 33He took Peter, James, and John with him, and he began to be filled with horror and deep distress. 34He told them, "My soul is crushed with grief to the point of death. Stay here and watch with me."

35He went on a little farther and fell face down on the ground. He prayed that, if it were possible, the awful hour awaiting him might pass him by. 36"Abba,* Father," he said, "everything is possible for you. Please take this cup of suffering away from me. Yet I want your will, not mine."

37Then he returned and found the disciples asleep. "Simon!" he said to Peter. "Are you asleep? Couldn't you stay awake and watch with me even one hour? 38Keep alert and pray. Otherwise temptation will overpower you. For though the spirit is willing enough, the body is weak."

39Then Jesus left them again and prayed, repeating his pleadings. 40Again he returned to them and found them sleeping, for they just couldn't keep their eyes open. And they didn't know what to say.

41When he returned to them the third time, he said, "Still sleeping? Still resting?* Enough! The time has come. I, the Son of Man, am betrayed into the hands of sinners. 42Up, let's be going. See, my betrayer is here!"

Jesus Is Betrayed and Arrested

43And immediately, as he said this, Judas, one of the twelve disciples, arrived with a mob that was armed with swords and clubs. They had been sent out by the leading priests, the teachers of religious law, and the other leaders.

14:27a Greek *I*. **14:27b** Zech 13:7. **14:36** *Abba* is an Aramaic term for "father." **14:41** Or *Sleep on, take your rest.*

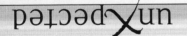

unXpected

LAVISH WORSHIP

It's a strange scene. An "overly emotional" woman takes a flask of exotic, expensive perfume and breaks it, pouring the substance on Jesus' feet. Her sudden, surprising actions bring a perfectly good dinner party to a screeching halt.

Almost before the valuable fragrance even has a chance to drip onto the floor, the more practical folks in attendance are scowling and complaining. The disruption. The mess. The waste.

But Jesus cuts them all off. He sees her actions for what they are: an act of absolute worship and love. He praises the woman, reminding us all that true adoration and thankfulness will often propel us to do crazy things, which others may criticize, but which heaven will applaud.

MARK 14:8

⁴⁴Judas had given them a prearranged signal: "You will know which one to arrest when I go over and give him the kiss of greeting. Then you can take him away under guard."

⁴⁵As soon as they arrived, Judas walked up to Jesus. "Teacher!" he exclaimed, and gave him the kiss. ⁴⁶Then the others grabbed Jesus and arrested him. ⁴⁷But someone pulled out a sword and slashed off an ear of the high priest's servant.

⁴⁸Jesus asked them, "Am I some dangerous criminal, that you come armed with swords and clubs to arrest me? ⁴⁹Why didn't you arrest me in the Temple? I was there teaching every day. But these things are happening to fulfill what the Scriptures say about me."

⁵⁰Meanwhile, all his disciples deserted him and ran away. ⁵¹There was a young man following along behind, clothed only in a linen nightshirt. When the mob tried to grab him, ⁵²they tore off his clothes, but he escaped and ran away naked.

Jesus before the Council
⁵³Jesus was led to the high priest's home where the leading priests, other leaders, and teachers of religious law had gathered. ⁵⁴Meanwhile, Peter followed far behind and then slipped inside the gates of the high priest's courtyard. For a while he sat with the guards, warming himself by the fire.

⁵⁵Inside, the leading priests and the entire high council* were trying to find witnesses who would testify against Jesus, so they could put him to death. But their efforts were in vain. ⁵⁶Many false witnesses spoke against him, but they contradicted each other. ⁵⁷Finally, some men stood up to testify against him with this lie: ⁵⁸"We heard him say, 'I will destroy this Temple made with human hands, and in three days I will build another, made without human hands.'" ⁵⁹But even then they didn't get their stories straight!

⁶⁰Then the high priest stood up before the others and asked Jesus, "Well, aren't you going to answer these charges? What do you have to say for yourself?" ⁶¹Jesus made no reply. Then the high priest asked him, "Are you the Messiah, the Son of the blessed God?"

⁶²Jesus said, "I am, and you will see me, the

temptation is strong, but there is someone stronger: Jesus. Trust him to see you through. (14:38)

Son of Man, sitting at God's right hand in the place of power and coming back on the clouds of heaven."*

⁶³Then the high priest tore his clothing to show his horror and said, "Why do we need other witnesses? ⁶⁴You have all heard his blasphemy. What is your verdict?" And they all condemned him to death.

⁶⁵Then some of them began to spit at him, and they blindfolded him and hit his face with their fists. "Who hit you that time, you prophet?" they jeered. And even the guards were hitting him as they led him away.

Peter Denies Jesus
⁶⁶Meanwhile, Peter was below in the courtyard. One of the servant girls who worked for the high priest ⁶⁷noticed Peter warming himself at the fire. She looked at him closely and then said, "You were one of those with Jesus, the Nazarene."

⁶⁸Peter denied it. "I don't know what you're talking about," he said, and he went out into the entryway. Just then, a rooster crowed.*

⁶⁹The servant girl saw him standing there and began telling the others, "That man is definitely one of them!" ⁷⁰Peter denied it again.

A little later some other bystanders began saying to Peter, "You must be one of them because you are from Galilee."

⁷¹Peter said, "I swear by God, I don't know this man you're talking about." ⁷²And immediately the rooster crowed the second time. Suddenly, Jesus' words flashed through Peter's mind: "Before the rooster crows twice, you will deny me three times." And he broke down and cried.

15

Jesus' Trial before Pilate
Very early in the morning the leading priests, other leaders, and teachers of religious law—the entire high

14:55 Greek *the Sanhedrin.* 14:62 See Ps 110:1; Dan 7:13. 14:68 Some manuscripts do not include *Just then, a rooster crowed.*

council*—met to discuss their next step. They bound Jesus and took him to Pilate, the Roman governor.

²Pilate asked Jesus, "Are you the King of the Jews?"

Jesus replied, "Yes, it is as you say."

³Then the leading priests accused him of many crimes, ⁴and Pilate asked him, "Aren't you going to say something? What about all these charges against you?" ⁵But Jesus said nothing, much to Pilate's surprise.

⁶Now it was the governor's custom to release one prisoner each year at Passover time—anyone the people requested. ⁷One of the prisoners at that time was Barabbas, convicted along with others for murder during an insurrection. ⁸The mob began to crowd in toward Pilate, asking him to release a prisoner as usual. ⁹"Should I give you the King of the Jews?" Pilate asked. ¹⁰(For he realized by now that the leading priests had arrested Jesus out of envy.) ¹¹But at this point the leading priests stirred up the mob to demand the release of Barabbas instead of Jesus. ¹²"But if I release Barabbas," Pilate asked them, "what should I do with this man you call the King of the Jews?"

¹³They shouted back, "Crucify him!"

¹⁴"Why?" Pilate demanded. "What crime has he committed?"

But the crowd only roared the louder, "Crucify him!"

¹⁵So Pilate, anxious to please the crowd, released Barabbas to them. He ordered Jesus flogged with a lead-tipped whip, then turned him over to the Roman soldiers to crucify him.

The Soldiers Mock Jesus

¹⁶The soldiers took him into their headquarters* and called out the entire battalion. ¹⁷They dressed him in a purple robe and made a crown of long, sharp thorns and put it on his head. ¹⁸Then they saluted, yelling, "Hail! King of the Jews!" ¹⁹And they beat him on the head with a stick, spit on him, and dropped to their knees in mock worship. ²⁰When they were finally tired of mocking him, they took off the purple robe and put his own clothes on him again. Then they led him away to be crucified.

The Crucifixion

²¹A man named Simon, who was from Cyrene,* was coming in from the country just

15:1 Greek *the Sanhedrin;* also in 15:43. 15:16 Greek *the courtyard, which is the praetorium.* 15:21 *Cyrene* was a city in northern Africa.

unXpected

GOOD INTENTIONS

Peter had clearly had enough of all the talk of Jesus being left high and dry at his hour of greatest need. "I won't!" he asserted. "Everyone else—maybe so. But not me. Never!"

You'd think Jesus would be warmed by Peter's bold talk and encouraged by his profession of loyalty. You'd expect him to at least smile weakly and say, "Thanks, Peter. I appreciate the support."

Instead Jesus looked his big-talking follower in the eyes and declared flatly, "No, the truth is, Peter, you'll deny me in a heartbeat. By morning it will be a done deal."

This is a stark reminder that good intentions are not enough against great temptation. Instead, we need to pray, seek help from others, and focus on following God's plan for our life.

MARK 14:30

then, and they forced him to carry Jesus' cross. (Simon is the father of Alexander and Rufus.) [22]And they brought Jesus to a place called Golgotha (which means Skull Hill). [23]They offered him wine drugged with myrrh, but he refused it. [24]Then they nailed him to the cross. They gambled for his clothes, throwing dice* to decide who would get them.

[25]It was nine o'clock in the morning when the crucifixion took place. [26]A signboard was fastened to the cross above Jesus' head, announcing the charge against him. It read: "The King of the Jews." [27]Two criminals were crucified with him, their crosses on either side of his.* [29]And the people passing by shouted abuse, shaking their heads in mockery. "Ha! Look at you now!" they yelled at him. "You can destroy the Temple and rebuild it in three days, can you? [30]Well then, save yourself and come down from the cross!"

[31]The leading priests and teachers of religious law also mocked Jesus. "He saved others," they scoffed, "but he can't save himself! [32]Let this Messiah, this king of Israel, come down from the cross so we can see it and believe him!" Even the two criminals who were being crucified with Jesus ridiculed him.

The Death of Jesus
[33]At noon, darkness fell across the whole land until three o'clock. [34]Then, at that time Jesus called out with a loud voice, *"Eloi, Eloi, lema sabachthani?"* which means, "My God, my God, why have you forsaken me?"* [35]Some of the bystanders misunderstood and thought he was calling for the prophet Elijah. [36]One of them ran and filled a sponge with sour wine, holding it up to him on a stick so he could drink. "Leave him alone. Let's see whether Elijah will come and take him down!" he said.

[37]Then Jesus uttered another loud cry and breathed his last. [38]And the curtain in the Temple was torn in two, from top to bottom. [39]When the Roman officer who stood facing him saw how he had died, he exclaimed, "Truly, this was the Son of God!"

[40]Some women were there, watching from a distance, including Mary Magdalene, Mary (the mother of James the younger and of Joseph*), and Salome. [41]They had been followers of Jesus and had cared for him while he was in Galilee. Then they and many other women had come with him to Jerusalem.

Punching God

It's hard to stomach this scene. Big, burly soldiers taking out their boredom and frustration on Jesus. For ten minutes or an hour, no one knows, they treat him like a human punching bag. Whatever sadistic ideas pop into their heads, this is what these goons proceed to do. The goal of each is to do something more violent and more degrading than the soldier before.

What is amazing here is that it is *God* they are spitting on, the *Creator* they are slapping across the face and cursing. And yet Almighty God just takes it, takes their most vicious punches and slumps heavily in a heap on the marble floor.

MARK 15:19

Xtraordinary **BUT TRUE**

15:24 Greek *casting lots*. See Ps 22:18. **15:27** Some manuscripts add verse 28, *And the Scripture was fulfilled that said, "He was counted among those who were rebels."* See Isa 53:12. **15:34** Ps 22:1. **15:40** Greek *Joses;* also in 15:47. See Matt 27:56.

The Burial of Jesus

⁴²This all happened on Friday, the day of preparation,* the day before the Sabbath. As evening approached, ⁴³an honored member of the high council, Joseph from Arimathea (who was waiting for the Kingdom of God to come), gathered his courage and went to Pilate to ask for Jesus' body. ⁴⁴Pilate couldn't believe that Jesus was already dead, so he called for the Roman military officer in charge and asked him. ⁴⁵The officer confirmed the fact, and Pilate told Joseph he could have the body. ⁴⁶Joseph bought a long sheet of linen cloth, and taking Jesus' body down from the cross, he wrapped it in the cloth and laid it in a tomb that had been carved out of the rock. Then he rolled a stone in front of the entrance. ⁴⁷Mary Magdalene and Mary the mother of Joseph saw where Jesus' body was laid.

16 *The Resurrection*

The next evening, when the Sabbath ended, Mary Magdalene and Salome and Mary the mother of James went out and purchased burial spices to put on Jesus' body. ²Very early on Sunday morning,* just at sunrise, they came to the tomb. ³On the way they were discussing who would roll the

Ever feel forgotten? Forsaken? Talk to Jesus. He knows the feeling. (15:34)

stone away from the entrance to the tomb. ⁴But when they arrived, they looked up and saw that the stone—a very large one—had already been rolled aside. ⁵So they entered the tomb, and there on the right sat a young man clothed in a white robe. The women were startled, ⁶but the angel said, "Do not be so surprised. You are looking for Jesus, the Nazarene, who was crucified. He isn't here! He has been raised from the dead! Look, this is where they laid his body. ⁷Now go and give this message to his disciples, including Peter: Jesus is going ahead of you to Galilee. You will see him there, just as he told you before he died!" ⁸The women fled from the tomb, trembling and bewildered, saying nothing to anyone because they were too frightened to talk.*

[*Shorter Ending of Mark*]

Then they reported all these instructions briefly to Peter and his companions. Afterward

15:42 Greek *on the day of preparation.* 16:2 Greek *on the first day of the week;* also in 16:9. 16:8 The most reliable early manuscripts conclude the Gospel of Mark at verse 8. Other manuscripts include various endings to the Gospel. Two of the more noteworthy endings are printed here.

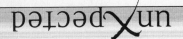

un✗pected

LIFTED UP

At last Jesus is lifted high where all can see. He wears a crown. A sign proclaims him king. He has something of a retinue around him. A group of onlookers kneel at his feet.

But things are not what they seem. His lofty perch is a Roman cross—an instrument of slow, agonizing death. The crown and the sign? Only evil, cruel "jokes." His "retinue"? Petty criminals—also sentenced to die. The group at his feet? Soldiers rolling dice to see which will get Jesus' robe.

On that terrible day we call Good Friday, Jesus was the recipient of ultimate indignity and rejection. His response? To forgive to the bitter end—and beyond!

MARK 15:27-32

Jesus himself sent them out from east to west with the sacred and unfailing message of salvation that gives eternal life. Amen.

[Longer Ending of Mark]

[9]It was early on Sunday morning when Jesus rose from the dead, and the first person who saw him was Mary Magdalene, the woman from whom he had cast out seven demons. [10]She went and found the disciples, who were grieving and weeping. [11]But when she told them that Jesus was alive and she had seen him, they didn't believe her.

[12]Afterward he appeared to two who were walking from Jerusalem into the country, but they didn't recognize him at first because he had changed his appearance. [13]When they realized who he was, they rushed back to tell the others, but no one believed them.

[14]Still later he appeared to the eleven disciples as they were eating together. He rebuked them for their unbelief—their stubborn refusal to believe those who had seen him after he had risen.

[15]And then he told them, "Go into all the world and preach the Good News to everyone, everywhere. [16]Anyone who believes and is baptized will be saved. But anyone who refuses to believe will be condemned. [17]These signs will accompany those who believe: They will cast out demons in my name, and they will speak new languages.* [18]They will be able to handle snakes with safety, and if they drink anything poisonous, it won't hurt them. They will be able to place their hands on the sick and heal them."

[19]When the Lord Jesus had finished talking with them, he was taken up into heaven and sat down in the place of honor at God's right hand. [20]And the disciples went everywhere and preached, and the Lord worked with them, confirming what they said by many miraculous signs.

16:17 Or *new tongues*. Some manuscripts omit *new*.

you have real questions...
And Jesus has real answers!

Now that you've Xperienced *The Jesus Bible*'s book of Mark, sample the Real Life...Real Questions...Real Jesus devotional series from Empowered Youth Products® and Standard Publishing.

Each of the four new 30-day devotionals for young adults includes material taken exclusively from *The Jesus Bible*.

A four-session Leader's Guide is also available for each devotional.

Sooner or later (and usually sooner, rather than later), every Christian doubts.

On the one hand, we've got this faith that makes spectacular claims, a faith based on an ancient book filled with jaw-dropping stories. On the other hand, we experience life in a world that has its share of wonder and beauty, but a world also filled with confusion and pain.

BELIEFS AND DOUBTS

We enjoy fleeting "Aha!" moments when Jesus seems so real; we feel as though we're peeking into heaven itself. At other times, if we're honest, the whole God thing seems like a cruel joke.

When times of doubt come (and believe it—they will come!), Christians tend to get very unnerved. After all, doubt is unchristian, isn't it? How can we call ourselves believers when we're questioning *what* or *if* we really believe? Christianity is all about *trusting.* Try counting the number of times the words "faith," "believe," and "trust" occur throughout the Bible, and you begin to get the idea that doubt is *not* the ideal for the so-called child of God.

Yet we do doubt. We're—some of us all the time, and all of us some of the time—exactly like the poor guy in the Bible who cried out to Jesus, "I do believe; but help me not to doubt!" (Mark 9:24). So the question is: What do we do in those dark moments when doubt seems to have the upper hand?

Two things: We realize doubt is normal. We remember that the most godly Christians in history, including the heroes we read about in the Bible, *all* struggled with doubt. Even John the

Baptist, the one described by Jesus as the greatest man ever born (Luke 7:28), was a certified doubter. Sitting in a prison cell, after a long ministry of announcing to anyone who would listen that Jesus *is* the Messiah, John had a faith crisis. He actually sent messengers to ask Jesus, "Are you *really* the one sent from God?"

Second, we let our doubts and questions prompt us to an even deeper search for Jesus. Rather than being a bad thing, honest doubts are, in the words of Frederick Buechner, "the ants in the pants of faith. They keep it alive and moving."

DAY 8 I meet the Jesus Challenge when I grow in my faith through my doubts.

Jesus knew what they were thinking, so he said, "Why are you so worried about having no food? Won't you ever learn or understand? Are your hearts too hard to take it in? 'You have eyes—can't you see? You have ears—can't you hear?' Don't you remember anything at all?"

Mark 8:17-18

REAL Xpressions

Faithless in Fresno

Something bad happened to me on our youth group's mission trip to Mexico. It's something I haven't told any-one, not even my parents or my youth leader.

We were in Mexico to build a house for a mother and her three kids. When we got to the building site, I couldn't believe what I was seeing. It was in the middle of a desert, next to a house made out of cardboard boxes, and no more than twenty yards away from the place where everyone in the area dumped their garbage and sewage. The smell was almost unbearable, and there were flies everywhere.

What killed me, though, was the way the woman and her children acted. They smiled the whole time we were there. They were so excited they could hardly wait for us to get done. Every time we finished a wall or a floor, the mother would say, "Praise the Lord," and then pray in Spanish.

I couldn't understand how she could be so happy and so thankful living in such a disgusting place.

The question that kept running through my mind was "Where was God?" I mean, here was a woman who obviously loved him, and he was letting her and her kids live in complete poverty!

The more I thought about it, the more confused I got. I felt like I was seeing God in a different way—and I didn't like what I saw. I started to question things I've always believed. I started to wonder whether God really loves us as much as we think he does.

Now I've got all kinds of doubts going through my head, and I don't know what to do. I feel like Thomas, that disciple who doubted Jesus.

I talked with my youth leader, and she said having doubts is OK, but to keep looking for answers and to remember that God can be trusted.

I can do that.

Walter

REAL QUESTION

Writer Mark Twain described faith as, "Believing what you know ain't so." Was he right? Is faith only for illogical people who ignore the harsh realities of life? Does faith mean that we put our minds on the shelf and immediately shove aside any uncomfortable facts or questions about God?

Can a person who loves God ever have doubts? And, if so, what do we do when we feel like Walter?

REAL ANSWER

Doubt seems to be a universal experience— even in the hearts and minds of those who love God deeply. Go down the biblical list of great saints: Abraham, Moses, David, the prophets, John the Baptist, the disciples, the apostle Paul—*all* experienced spiritual dark times when they questioned *everything* about their faith. Realize this is normal.

So what do you do in those uncomfortable moments? As trite as it sounds, you defeat doubt as you experience God through faith in Jesus Christ. It's a growth curve thing. You can't act like a middle-schooler during your college years. You've got to keep on growing. To use another metaphor, faith is like a muscle that is either being strengthened through rigorous exercise or wasting away through non-use. The point is, the life of faith never stands still.

But "I doubt *everything*!" you say. "When can I begin to believe again?" If your mind is full of doubt, at least you're certain about this: You know the hunger of wanting to know more. Start there. Pray for faith to take God at his word (Mark 9:24). God loves the thinker, the feeler, the seeker, the person hungry to know more. Learn about God through a study of the Bible and its doubters. Trust God one step at a time, one day at a time. Concentrate on trusting him *in this moment*.

Is doubt ever beaten entirely? Some people confess that doubt never pesters them. Others admit to lingering doubts even after years of following Jesus. The doubt you feel is a reminder to trust and depend on God until the day you die—then you'll experience God's presence firsthand.

Rest in God's promise, secured for you in Jesus Christ. Surrender your doubts to God. Take the step of faith and watch God work.

REAL YOU

Even though Jesus calls me to faith—to trust without reservation, to believe even when I can't see the outcome—I know I will still encounter situations where I will be tempted to doubt. If everything were obvious and clear and understandable all the time, I would have no need for faith. Current situations that test the depths of my faith are:

_____

_____

_____

_____

_____

_____

_____

Some situations in my life in which I have strongly seen God give my faith a shot in the arm include . . .

_____

_____

_____

_____

_____

_____

_____

_____

_____

X ALTED

Truth

For centuries, people have asked, "what is truth?" The dictionary defines it as that which is fact, actual, and real—and which is therefore accurate, reliable, and trustworthy. In John's Gospel, Jesus declares himself to be the Truth (John 14:6). Jesus is the real deal! He is reliable. Depend on that fact and on him.

Relationships. Everybody's got 'em. (Duh!) You can't live on this earth without having a relationship of some kind. Some relationships you're born into. Others—those with friends, for instance—you choose yourself. Even though you didn't choose your mom or your Uncle Fred, you can choose *how* you relate to each person. Some relationships will be deeper than others of course, unless you're the kind of person who has nothing but really, really close family and friends. ("I'd like to thank my two thousand best friends for this award.")

RELATIONSHIPS

The way you relate in any relationship comes from your experience with Jesus—how much you understand his love for you. Want to know how non-Christians should tell who the Christians are? Love. Love, according to Jesus, should be the hallmark of his followers (John 13:35).

The fact that we have relationships at all can be traced back to God. He created us to enjoy relationships. ("It is not good for the man to be alone"—Genesis 2:18.) Because God loves us, we can love others. That's the truth, plain and simple. You don't even need to read any further. Just kidding!

Just like snowflakes, no two relationships are the same. They're all unique. But some relationships share characteristics in common. Some might bring you more joy than others. Others might seem more trouble than they're worth. One thing is for sure: all relationships take work. And every once in a while, you might need a word or two of advice. Where can you get the help you need to handle your relationships? The Bible is a manual for relationships. If you're a believer, you also have a built-in advice counselor you can access quicker than Dr. Laura. He's the Holy Spirit.

God wants to do more than just hear about your relationships. He wants to be involved in them. Want to experience Jesus in your relationships? Read on.

 **DAY** I find the Jesus Experience when I trust in God's plan for sex.

But God's plan was seen from the beginning of creation, for "He made them male and female." "This explains why a man leaves his father and mother and is joined to his wife, and the two are united into one." Since they are no longer two but one, let no one separate them, for God has joined them together.

Mark 10:6-9

real Xpressions

White Wedding

My friends think the reason I'm still a virgin is that I want to be able to wear white on my wedding day. Can you believe that? Like I have some kind of superstition about the color of my wedding gown. I told them that if that were true, I would have had sex a long time ago. Hey, if sex were as good as everybody says it is, I'd have tried it even if it meant I had to wear a plaid wedding dress.

What I'm doing *is* waiting for something better than "good." I'm waiting for something perfect. I know that God's plan for the ultimate loving relationship—a husband and wife giving themselves totally to each other—beats anything my friends talk about. And I'm willing to wait as long as necessary to make sure that I get that kind of relationship.

Some of my friends say they sleep with their boyfriends because they "love" them. But when I hear guys talk about it, it's like love is the last thing on their mind. And what happens when they break up? (Which they *always* do.) It's like the sex between them loses all of its meaning.

I don't want that to happen with me. I don't want to ever have to worry about whether the guy I give my virginity to loves me or not. I want to know that we can enjoy sex with each other for the rest of our lives. That's why I'm going to do things according to God's timetable.

Kelsey

real question

Did Jesus say that sex before marriage is wrong?

Think about the shows or movies you've seen recently. According to society, what are the ingredients that make a good dating relationship? Are these on your list?

For many people, sex is an automatic ingredient of a relationship. Many people believe that sex just naturally follows "love" and don't believe that they need to put any limits on how they express that love with their significant other.

So, why is wearing a white wedding gown so important to Kelsey? Is this important to you? Would you want this to be important to your future spouse and your future kids?

real answer

Sex is one of the most talked about subjects around. There's nothing wrong with sex. After all, God invented it. But with God, there is a purpose for everything.

As recorded in the Gospel of Mark, Jesus quoted from Genesis 1:27 and 2:24 to remind his listeners of God's design for marriage. Two people would become one. This isn't a magician's trick. It shows the level of intimacy two people share. Sex is the physical expression of that intimacy. It is not meant to be cheapened by the experimentation of two people who aren't even sure they like each other. It is also not a bargaining chip to be used to hold on to a relationship.

Paul, one of Jesus' followers and the author of most of the New Testament, knew God's plan for marriage. That's why he could strongly urge the readers of First Corinthians to "run away from sexual sin" (1 Corinthians 6:18). He brought this up about five times in this letter and in other letters. (See Romans 13:13; 1 Corinthians 6:13; 10:8.) In 1 Thessalonians 4:3-5, Paul tells us to be different from the world. Does this mean that sex is wrong? No way. But sex outside of God's plan is. God created you, he created sex, and he knows what's best for you. If you will be patient and wait on God, who has a plan for your life, he will work it out for you. His plan includes all areas of your life, including your romantic life—especially your sex life. God may choose to call you to a life of singleness, so that you can be fully devoted to him (see 1 Corinthians 7:1; 32-35). If he does that, he will give you the peace to accept it.

REAL YOU

This is what I've always believed about sex before or after marriage:

_____

_____

_____

_____

_____

_____

_____

_____

_____

_____

_____

_____

_____

_____

_____

_____

_____

This is what I would tell my friends about God's design for marriage:

_____

_____

_____

_____

_____

_____

_____

_____

_____

_____

_____

_____

_____

_____

_____

_____

_____

_____

_____

_____

_____

_____

_____

Χalted

Mighty Power

Who is the most powerful person you
know? A corporate CEO? The president of the
United States? Your best friend? Paul described
Jesus as a "mighty power" (2 Corinthians 13:3). That
means he can do anything. When you're facing temptation, a corporate CEO can't do much for you except pray
that God will help you. When you need *real* power to handle
tough situations and temptations, remember to go straight to the
Source, Jesus. He will help you overcome (1 Corinthians 10:13).

A Note to Readers

Since its early years, Tyndale House Publishers has been committed to publishing editions of the Bible in the language of the people. With over forty million copies in print, *The Living Bible* represented this tradition well for more than thirty years. More recently, Tyndale has continued this tradition by commissioning ninety evangelical scholars to produce the *Holy Bible*, New Living Translation. This general-purpose translation is accurate and excellent for study, while also being easy to read. The NLT is helping many discover, and rediscover, the power of God's living Word.

The goal of any translation of the Scriptures is to convey the meaning of the ancient Hebrew and Greek texts as accurately as possible to the contemporary reader. The challenge for our translators was to create a text that would make the same impact in the lives of modern readers that the original text did in the lives of readers in its ancient context. In the New Living Translation, this has been accomplished by translating entire thoughts (rather than just words) into natural, everyday English. The end result is a translation that is easy to read and understand and that accurately communicates the meaning of the original texts.

We believe that the New Living Translation, which combines the latest in scholarship with the best in translation style, will speak to your heart. We publish it with the prayer that God will use it to speak his timeless truth to the church and to the world in a fresh and powerful way.

The Publishers
July 1996

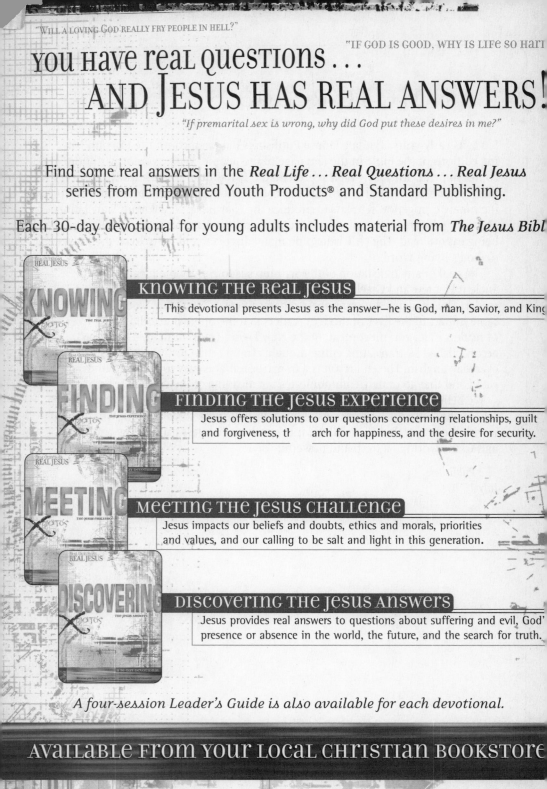

"WILL A LOVING GOD REALLY FRY PEOPLE IN HELL?"

"IF GOD IS GOOD, WHY IS LIFE SO HARD

YOU HAVE REAL QUESTIONS . . .
AND JESUS HAS REAL ANSWERS!

"If premarital sex is wrong, why did God put these desires in me?"

Find some real answers in the *Real Life . . . Real Questions . . . Real Jesus*
series from Empowered Youth Products® and Standard Publishing.

Each 30-day devotional for young adults includes material from *The Jesus Bibl*

KNOWING THE REAL JESUS

This devotional presents Jesus as the answer—he is God, man, Savior, and King

FINDING THE JESUS EXPERIENCE

Jesus offers solutions to our questions concerning relationships, guilt
and forgiveness, th   arch for happiness, and the desire for security.

MEETING THE JESUS CHALLENGE

Jesus impacts our beliefs and doubts, ethics and morals, priorities
and values, and our calling to be salt and light in this generation.

DISCOVERING THE JESUS ANSWERS

Jesus provides real answers to questions about suffering and evil, God'
presence or absence in the world, the future, and the search for truth.

A four-session Leader's Guide is also available for each devotional.

AVAILABLE FROM YOUR LOCAL CHRISTIAN BOOKSTORE

meet the Real Jesus

See His Passion

Sense His Presence

Feel His Love

Open the pages of the *Jesus Bible* and come face to face with the Savior. Learn un✗pected facts about Jesus. Connect with others just like you by reading their Real ✗pressions. ✗alt Him through all the names, titles, and descriptions of Jesus. And ✗plicit Answers will point you to solutions to life's toughest problems.

The *Jesus Bible*.

Available wherever Bibles are sold.

NEW LIVING TRANSLATION

for those who thirst.

TYNDALE

www.newlivingtranslation.com